gutter 's

Gutters

harry k stammer

Sandy Press

gutter 's

Cover design, cover preparation, & interior layout by

harry k stammer

ISBN: 979-8-9924582-2-0

Printed in U.S.A.

Sandy Press

Sandy-press.com

Thanks for the continuing support from Mark Young, Eileen Tabios, Mark
Cunningham, George Meyers and Heath Brougher

Some of the pieces have appeared in ē· rā/ tiō, #Ranger and warnell.com/library

Contents

Once the part starts to grate the grating begins…

Jim

Jim dropped a hammer a

Dingy barks at a tree a

Jim picked up the hammer and squinted a

Mary realizes the cup is not full a

"stop jumping around" a

down the sidewalk is a street a

Mary drops her keys a

cans in the street, a

June night in, a

sliding in Mary coughed, a

some muddy hole, a hole, a

Dingy sniffed the air, a

blub, a

"Seth, how do you feel about your toddler years?" a

thought Jim, a

after the rains

some calm... a

walking away Seth, a

cigarette smoke, a

Jim said, though parked away, a

rolling the window down, a

Seth holds Dingy, a

screen door opens, in comes Jim, a

stopping, a clack, clack, clack, a

a clacka, clacka

clacka, claka, clk, a

the bag Jim puts on, a

Seth sits, a

Dingy click clacks, a

the a/c came on, a

80 degrees, a

Seth thinks salamander fire, a

mystery isn't a, a with Dingy, a walkway, a

Seth can't hear, a

Dingy paws at Jim's door, a

a gun shot, another, a

Seth whisked two eggs, a

Seth eats eggs, Dingy licks a paw, a

twelve

said "break but" (pales) and punch

does (nt) wait "close't" separate where 2 rail't

basis "get in" along a past (liner)

peddle yet's hang a rule around'd say "all"

a simple basis (instant) reasoning'd a gate

change it "basis" and technique a patch of

(d) wearing long and shiny stringy saying

"is carried" sack in bags' easy luck

blue (not)'d's a 'traction at every's out

back saying "hey, jeans!" bottle up out in

blue's 'sequences turn out in up up's

sands bound'd singing a sing a sing (ing)

red'ss esque that float while a baking

misty (morn) an altitude none or one

less angled up/down saying "dripping to" west

risen't grayish as yellow glints's its best

patient, wait'a crawl an't slowly saying "I smell't"

against wall floor broken (once there)

sure find't middle aisles rolling else some

that one (tubing's)'t twist a straight wrist

say 4

before 3 ten miles to a

say 4 before 3 again until (hurting)

begins crumbs falling (to) floor no vacuum here

break your leg and set it down

saying "well" we'll turn point 'thing ratio'd

saying "er..." wheel package wells shift'd

'says berries little'r berry solid equal trails out

said "see that hole?" steel head trout

rainbow (s) drain where fish saying "but"

eyes shadow (d) harm ing to moisture 'es

'nbows 'anbowd swirling 'wirling one (s) pepper

slapping rest of 'em s'rainbow (s)

fish

checked saying "take another turn" out
check'd said "take another turn" out there
say "take another turn" out there checking its
out there words a "take another turn"
theme tune; buried newspaper spilled't beer a
hind legs (rowing) direction pulled saying "that
icy sea" singing "burned it't" surface and
up singing "lanyard" well foam sink (t)
"ohhhh 'carnassus" two wheels 'vated six to

Ἁλικαρνασσοῦ 'trŭk'chər antss crawl cereal bowl slurpy'y

some milk east façade's say "get" dig
can off a ground playing'ly 'bria
packed to go (intervene) ing said "the
'piety" looked backing ass forward'd run fast

look "come close" t'know backseat /dəg/ one

shovel bumper sinking in driving out 'er
said "laughing" chances sped't a shifted are
said "hey…" Hómēros 'wall spot'd not seen
said "that" grātus ranges outward chance be
said "song" between four or five spokess

"perfectly

as" agreed's stirred in d'ed' 'nings
/spelt/ by finger tips ran across said
"you know" open windows open moved to
where air is feeling light as airs'
tracking particles (fair) and tiny says "point
a" dog a bird (stopped) tufted'd ether't a
c2 crawling (bubble)'t eyess' dug Mozart
addressed 216 times c2 as in Greece
two bulbs pairs that width span brown
hair three saying "thinking" why fearss' wrestle
kiss a foot playing sing "natural number"
put into pick a frequency between'd -5
"you struggle" collision better very'll which a
seen said "you" get access't toes radiated
"again to" increase between (ev'ry)'t feud'd
for once dents scrapes it less paint
check pulled seem said "hint" straight liner
a pole and it's spinner (ing) round'd
pull back 'nacker singing "play it once"
it rolls in/over't banging the rudder there

extraluminal

gas within the mediastinum gas may

originate from the lungs trachea central spelling

bronchi esophagus peritoneal cavity track from

the mediastinum to the neck or abdomen

strangled't saying "just pull" pull't hard

hair cuts (gain) said "can you see?"

surf rid'nt tumble strands hang return a

revengeful pastel sung "one bright day" date

if it's (access) blessed role said "she

will" not have namess' heard 'latory piece

or reflect brown (ish) with lashes 'ssschss

fall in place knife singing "those mirrors"

pits little bullet sized mm's "it doesn't

work" pits tiny saying both sized't 'like

pits olives braised lamb'ss pits dug as

work said "rent it" bury it all

come on

"it's the jerk

he's doing the fly

Don't play him cheap

'cause you know he ain't shy spelling

ge's doing the monkey, the mashed potato

jump back Jack, see the later alligator s

/kən'strikSH(ə)n/

intestinal say "to proceed with'd"

effort pull back your hairs let's

lessen let's shrink sing "break my heart"

/SHriNGk/'s your heart'd the spring sigh (ing)

end virus's (paling) lumps flowing a failure

one cliff tops be blowing (singing) "why

March?" fill in the boxes scratch scratch

fluids as through eaten away march on't

a jacket

says "died of scoliosis and not due to exhaustion of work" as

both present it

as actual tunnel steels sing "wheels a turn"

heats up gas downward some short arms

'terite "mama, it's been years" rake it

event pregnant in stated bob here bob

up maybe saying "owning a stake" action

less than two months ago would have

'no bath water no babies plucking eyebrows
slip say "once" sidewalksss' wet as slippery
"we are?" heel clicking rustle bag change
pocket (¢)'d another to are it straight?

eye ear throat singing "that's how he'll"

amen captain ceasing no ceasing small time

variance said "cruelty, don't" see how's hear

t'd scratches fine pencil pencil cruel sores

a target

"don't imagine" table wine food

a someone's disperse electrons flood viaduct

a cross throughout lone pieces trace'd backing

a break saying "spin up" throw it away

and, there are moments where: then it's,

"not me, paranoia's the garlic in life's

kitchen, right, you can never have too

much.-- TP", too much onion and oil

one spiral cap cast't bubble away burying

arm legs't said "practice" no cap emptiness

misty mountain topped (dusted) with a rivul'd

leg thought leaking all over the hall

blown top saying "so blue" so transparent'd

checked both road ways lost cornered as

chipped petal set said "butter knife" propane

no sleep no gates no watch it

dammit the view down as (above) signatures

paper said, "beautiful" yeah another TV shows

forget but capacity singing "lazy bastard" so

get up go out he'll see you

boil

twelve eat at noon ; bake

eleven minutes (pray)'d table out by 2

median opinion delete't and shuffle times 2

a while singing "tell the moon" humid

boil twelve eat at noon ; bake
eleven minutes (pray)'d table out by 2
median opinion delete't and shuffle times 2
a while singing "tell the moon" humid
singing "have a little, empathy" dragged body
steps blunt'd stair edge dragging (v) large
(ly) back up /brāk/ "touch" said blow
er's's rev it up parts bath tub
mince 'schmäusekrieg "it ends?" saying plug
them up leaking say "escape once" on
secondsss past (w) tail't stick point trail
waves twist past where sun downs drown'd
saying "dread a" thumb two majors one

finger singing "borrow some time" (ἀοιδός) ;

rock salt water stairs stab't (stan) "ah"
authority said "perfect" a cart a club

"tug at it"

rip't edge smokes where at

1 sing "tug it" lace'd two shoes

red then gray (none) sails there east in

chop (sy) redgray'd even foggy at times

/blənt/ and not usual as smashed screaming

"what?" eye floor table rolls over't said

pitched'd four liner three ends rhymed saying

"flatten" [OBJ]'t knife cut through deep singing

check "keep going" spills choke 'em balls

did sing "keep it going" spilling choking

all ballsss't resting (at) home "keep it

all going" spill't choked't pass it down

"distant traffic blaring" weak necks break weak

pale elbows outside (saying) like (said) leak

oil paint chipped up't shoe scuff 'er

weak "neck" horn ear close by it

"was it" said wrestle down (virtue) demand

spread't singing "the bodies" never mind

in dirt (ed) arms out carpet two

broken femurs singing "ahhhhgh" trails set up

take it

'xcret (gaunt) /gônt/ safe twoss

let's sing "all may" bit fatigue bite

blood (out) by scrap 'e "steep" tea

zero day "we drag" a bit'o milk

"elvis is alive" torn ligament knees injuries

"why?" orange cones (stick) never a lane

straight ahead transformss "cause a thing" singing leg ahead leg

behind leg (s)

talking "seal the bait" hook less J

fell over without any support any sun

up's fallen images not (eternity)'t holy

talking "seal the bait" hook less J

track (a) wrapped around tree fires

once assigned said "even" determines form (s)

singing "pesto pizzaz" search't good food as

transcendent purse and water on a cinder

walk back said "throughout" wood weedy and

dozens (of) sell'd "it" singing nose through

all mouthing breaks's slip "ah" granites all

along busy roads freeway off-ramp slides

poke

around stick spread't leaf removal or

pepper there sayings "parted" do less do

still "error" rake around't bubbling leaks or

since one "says" a pull them up

Seth looked down the hallway.

The room Jim was in was backlit below.

brains "all over" a wall. Seth stared.

took a day to (;) less a cup of

tea "don't" walk

walk the hallway two steps back front

door Charlie barks "hey"

outside that door the porch Charlie and

Seth ; "hey" bark

there is one vegetable that I can't eat no matter

how it's cooked, broiled, roasted, no matter how much

soy sauce,vinegar, hot sauce, salt and pepper,

it curls my taste buds the vegetable

bonded salivary glands with no call response

Seth

began to lose consciousness Charlie

licked Seth's face

/ˈkapt(ə)n/ Bun climb'd two steps up'd hand

"are you" tense there

up stairs /ˈkapt(ə)n/ Bun stood crack door

inch two

an inch revolver pushing "hey……. in there…"
Seth and Charlie walk

at 5th turning on to "bark" away

some sidewalks walks

the room and dead Jim /ˈkapt(ə)n/

bun looks tragic they called, "it's tragic" a tragedy

spotted dogs leash singing "long lost…" it

isn't no (a wreck) yes and wrecked

shouts "a bit of rusted steel" sand

blood on the wall (check'd) panels wood

cool hair dragging sing "paint" sex pint't in it

lags bending in it more said "bobbing

up down" three sides right stating "that"

areas's coming long sum of and blessings

watching

someone adjust right side glasse (s)
rest not sure "it's habit" a less
said left "upper" brings (er) balanced face
bleak news to a day in weeks

the lamp and Jim's hair'ss /ˈkapt(ə)n/ Bun

eyes "huh"
concrete edge to another "leak" down it
goes singing "grab" result or 'law's valleys
pieces the older staged "town" a horse
some trot others beg's said "a living"
check back "it's bourbon (y's)" perfect
lines's sing "leveeeee" /līnd/ of as it
to say "scratch" don't answer as it
says "downs" and said "no" back look
Charlie stopped Seth bent down picked a
speck off his shoe
Baxter followed down the hallway the
room past (the) kitchen counter stain'd
Baxter sees Jim less left than right
and the blood

breeding

a are it was "slipping" one

string set as to blue three red "does

this" the smooth asphalt

 bend (x-) vision sides each

side "here they!" around 15th to work

Seth stands up and thinks "the garden"

Charlie sniffs the speck

limp arm dropped Baxter knowsno pulse

singing "some salads" rest'd long away

/bôg,bäg/'s "sure" said go away saying bones

and rocks (the) touch feel grasses moss

eaten introduced slow's 'ging bare (ly) posing

Bob and Bryan in the garden shovels glove

Baxter looked at Sergeant Kath one eye

Another trust and wheel (o) sing "lawyer" to

as where when sung "eoooh" narrower's where

ringing "where'ss" touch a touch't spin back

"it's three or four" love the hair

faith

pepper (/) terrify (ing) saying (s)

"yes..." 'sume and early as it as

said "baking" (s) nothing stag·nant steps over

the salt and said "250" break it

cynical there that turn into an icecold water bath in "the" say a

little less 'ilthy "gates" opening a bet

ditch consequence degrees below to a uh

Sergeant Kath one eye another eyes

Baxter and frowns

that optimist four blows below the belt

screaming "waaaaa!" suggested an it a it'd

sagged sunk say "float" four feet less

three said "stop" what you said't to'

Bryan digs and Bob sits

one another some sandy

wry, ask "they go" (?,) grease ('y')

made [OBJ]certain squares make eh eh say

time "parallel" some gas a to 'em

tug'd pulled away coerced a few

Baxter

says to Kath
"the bell" looks (?)
Mary always called Charlie Dingy
confusing Seth
Charlie was Seth's ears
Mary mouthed Dingy
... tests (f) sing "pray" 'foot over mud
under mind't bugs step'd said "it's" bigger
maps one delay (ing)'t squishy squish say
"hey!" it's jar another within cloud asks
Baxter and Kath walk out to the street
Bob and Bryan dig some
cattle of the fourth "ah" tip mountain
(sing'g) bump posts' "made" train point it
canyon narrow'st here says "rub" char coal
bottles say "piss's" smoke me mom't nows
dig dig'ing Bob then Bryan slow crawl
"lacking this" song sing shoveling this grass
say "geo's" bag drag pain (t) field
related said "between" fill't and in it

say

"geo's" bag drag pain (t) field

related said "between" fill't and in it

dig dig'ing Bob then Bryan slow crawl

"lacking this" song sing shoveling this grass

"oops that's shit" Seth looks back at

the house no toddler

stretch outs .....)(reek full s

said "take" pull workin' there't 't 't

sing "parades" but it was not a

length as saying "set" set in s's

pull't in suck "ahhhd" target hits it

firm said "aaahhd" (tag) there once spec't

Bob pulls Jim into the hole Bryan

shoveling shoe drops pushing said (s) "that"

singing "try" it packs some bouncing (t) (d)

thuds axe whistling ducks't said "sneer" geese

quick one bounce parrots active the bulls

here says "er'ing" paint stirs rings

from

and end says "forward" gray (un)

to a tense nor is't blank 'cross

sing "widely" square said "brightly" pair (s)

wing dribble away lagging there as 'to

Bob says "not enough dirt" Bryan shrugs

and walks

ear eyeballs floor rolls edge outside's a

reaching says "boats" slap waves't slap't a

again see wood grains sing "on" a

sea around sand wooden carpet obstacle seems

Baxter and Kath walk by an

EMT whoosh

reach (x) s grade't say "turn" right

both under scapes' high chair as sing

"where" leaves higher body to inches as

each other (x)'s said "twelve" deep in

"the body?" EMT yelling Kath turns

"what?" say "signal" gain from the current location

tapered't have any more information getting

silvery sing "spot" difference in a single

trail'st in a row off echo up

Baxter says

"entropy, they don't understand."
Kath looks, "empathy?"
truck stops said "a" piece tires off
well singing "runaway" steps's off none now
more coffee'd changing blue "baby" says it
runs "flawed" decent's front wheel (s) go
checked (past)'s loop't sing "prize" bridge
mark't be on this smeared bloody says
"if" personal choice ($) drooping is the
say "then" no but's hurt pen mark'd
contacts too (: /)'s "palms" sing's out er
pats head arm and shoulders said "up"
organ of a human's (ist)'d crash victims
legs back seat front seat back window
seems a bit more than a normal
pickle (in) grip and pressed't sing "all"
try sensing up coast says "drain" (d)
concrete not flagstone there tumble a trips
spaces blanks sing "foggy" a pail gone
slips woods said "steps" volume is does
this spreads out alluvial'esque some scratch s
ants into the tiny hole flooded

Seth says

"scratchy" throat Charlie walksup the street

"Heigh, my hearts! Cheerly, cheerly, my hearts!"

Baxter and Kath set up a /pəˈrimədər/

around the house, Bob gets in the hole with Jim and

hovel blue tarp as cover

step step step process by says "ballast"

over over rolls'ngt pulses thump thump s

(s) sing "on" once trade pitch'd a

rock mass pull pull said roll over

spell "this" surrender say "hey!" brick a

cut mind place sing "crawl" sand slopes

bend in't tell "to" fears sing "no" a

long "but" pray it's (5) not three

powder irritate bowls sing "lanes" out outers

glare'n at stop tinkling sings it "open" toes

cuts to webs crawled (ly) spoke "now" tuck

legs twist in's said "lane" around there

slug slide "grab" yelling head concrete pops

sing "tender" dual as twins and spreads

slow say "blood" chug slips point hear't

in't even started to move on with

table

gun cutting "science" page s t

one guilt four finger nail said "bug"

a belt'd lossy hands pallet rods smokes

"sings" grazed saints scrawl'd two t s

return'd here to find a solution for

saying "pinch" sing "belts" out severed it

lower part waves over't s drag't less and

leg says "brace" just very much as

brand new pants say "feel" perfect legs

those grown aside from sing "them" anyone

toes (bending)'s tranquil middle knee meets t

buried walking slows said "shoes" tumble s

stringy peaks say "his" under counter kitchen

sing "1,2,3,4,uh,5" note bore batches muck skip

skips t said "blossom" a blood check

said "runs" pocket'd turn left over it

catch it "sailors" song sung drafting 'ere

saying "run" railing over't limes shit'and bilge

truck back in roller said "faster" then

no some says "too" take the first'n

arm

pull (said) brass's once historic since

says "are" drains (ing)'t slide top over

year sing "brains" all interests cans spilled

(t) "ding" past anatomical takes floor wood

saw horse an infect singing "paws" up

anchors canvas drops said "short" tough muscle

setting north run'd shout "run" though it

doesn't no moisture's say "broke" arm bone

plants there is no evidence that sick

plants in a tree lined'd with square

plants control sing "next" emerge in as

plants saying "one" one a dead (em)

Seth and Charlie run up the stairs lead lack

a paper doors, mulch

pull spar back scream "pull" slipping't get

to scream pull "back" wood chip bloody hands

screaming "pull" over your face while holding

s'bare arms in roll a roll and pull

Seth says "you"

know Charlie/Dingy

the table does bend (t)

muscle tuck it singing "sling" hear at

tensors (don't) say "for" and it sounds

'tension fog is (5) to long sun's

'flict "yes" said at puuush a on

Jim's fingers move grasp a finger

Bob screams a

targets event sing "just" vary airs from

cut some loss say "edges" said step

trail a gravel fence bits sticks foot

tip say "last" one now another go Jim wakes up

thinking "don't dance cause it's in D"

impedance get "back" says 'ency gives eyes

singing "no" where is that at all

pass't over gravely has bleed none says

"backs" fluent pattern down as slow as

what "sets" sing another one rooms t

h ux jawing "in" turds out out

cabbages's out out purples saying "ask"

barns fire ruins shouting "get" out now

character

pit smoke says "no" perfect't close

toenails (less)'u bled sing "skin" removed from

evidence s f t wet drains ways

'sery missing weighted pull'd by a hole(s)

Jim brushed the dirt off

turned and walked

shred s the fanned over make singing

"special" just wrecked much (will)'s the

pains to no thing saying "here" duckcross't

 fouls calls "there" touch d piece

"run" (s)'s say some pounds away in

round'd in sides sing "six" paired to

circle't walk in to get to a's

swing door spins (h)'s trunk close t

pokes verse'ss (56)'s "ring" it up knew

push'd test test shriekss "oh" or something

poke 'erable shade azure'esque spread s o

push again reds float'd pencil pusher "rings"

Sid sees Jim waving the window

as a good view through

purr (s)

switch say "bag't" much shorter

pairs hang (ing)'t sing "give" letter a

put it to (8)'s prayers ash t

pail dropped feed on a small toe

stack't rolled up paper say "slap" down

a side an outer "slap" against end

strayss inky and did not (f)ly't sing

"slap" pull bench raze said "these" bare

bread say "bread" then sing "oil" t

matters had 'excur up into see through

pinch't spread out over here this says

"tomato" meat tortilla s beg "no" thing

can'd broken saying "all" whips down down

foggy can'd splayed singing "none" those nooses

down down can'd but cleaners worms water

down down down said "all" lose them

x c i bullet it with the

other x c i says "oh" and

x c i bullets are not in

say "oh" non back x c i

much

"ohss" with a bit more detail

speaks "ized" and "ohss" eye ball in'a

linoleum flax seedss ants little sing "ized's"

flat cheeks arms and twists as "ohss"'s

much say "get" a hit sin gels

equal'ss contrail sing "eight" 'tget to in

more's a chance g ta burnss' saids

or just plain water spray at it

dig holes dig singing "dig" holes ok

palms many though bent said "fronds" ok

open the said "shackle" fanci- (less) uh

hole digging say "as" pick a key

sleep minute make "it" say intent on

some a chalk (s) line'd b o's

locks sing "troubles" in 'sequent less walk

past hour train with said "it" over

different 'sa "bells" (Venice reference) 'sa 'sa

peck t s hang back n get

sing "bells" (threes) s t range ridge

blow "planesss" curling ly moist air downs'

brushes's

deep and brownish't fell (ing) t
says "crush" 'neutic pressure in sides t
sings "me" wavy memory walls't's climb t
broom pour rinse a said "please" don t
'ust'a flap wing say "gray" on was't
striped aheads white skullsss phase letter e
sing "over" horizons on on's making a
looms "heads" said beaks three up r
piles saying "ah" small pecking tap tap
breaks tap splinters't sing "ahsss" little glass a
piece (cake) chocolates tiny tiny surface s
ing said "says" dishes are set drops.
bugs are a big deal says "eel"
at to spin 16 holes sing "'lebby"
damns in feet run (another) yelling "flegs"'t
slow climb to crawls slide "as't" insects
vents up a yellowish t said "disturb"
one there place singing "all" (all) of
(Roman era reference) agate 'arble m a
saying that "catch" m'ings on the floor

gloomy

fogs be g hold up sing'g

"lower" granite bench mark says a "ah"

that a that a "yes" sings back'g

tonight slides behind foggy a yell "AH!"

shouts "no" new complete sentence said "no"

twirl'n romantic'd lil beach chairs sandss memory

singing "noooo" much past't dribble none at

no times exhibit times no say no

itchy red soreness's gang ant said "trub"

s pinch in inner plates say "sure"

thing to shepherd to nailed't backwards "draw"

sings it wiped wipes angry hoof s

concrete tent asphalt weed shit piss trash

a tents a were as said "green"

elbow says "'ture" three state s round

cup towels cut through plastic sings "are"

elbow says "'ture" three state s round

concrete tent asphalt weed shit piss trash

cup towels cut through plastic sings "are"

a tents a were as said "green"

two

cinder block slip around say "wait"

step downs thumb singing "what?" nail backs

crush forearm concrete tent asphalt weed shit piss trash cup

 towels cut through plastic

two for circulate stare "smooth" a bore

s 'olid portions see "ball" rolls round't

before during moment relief saw "shine" s

t and staged to run heads 's

shows (in) which scream "fires" drips in

damp say "air" blue and flame s

'bility tip t to sing "sure" fill

all top'r at point it can drained

pickle'd jars stack sing "pause" drive street

bigger say "yep" it's pickle d less

said "noise" but juggle't walk around roads

a device fitting "there" to the east

grunt'd blows sing "ass" on highways there

strangled onion root'd says "s" wave wind

see (horizon)s swell hills rise thigh s

said "s" spread here on a too's

sigh

"um" slides as pull muddy pat

pat mumble "um" buckle s tight n

singing "um" tapping a clod off of

says "ah" cuffing plug't said anything s

shows a number "3" yeah ok's it

spongy clumpy sing "unload" yeah ok's it

sink a towel a number "6" yeah

ok's it yell "jump" drop s it

sticking packs up say "leave" one portion

working's pick up two or three'a say

"now" background focus get a thought o

stick back singing "hole" blood wet r

punch holes (stage)'s wood a dust dirt

shout "target" flat head again walled't's and

punch't hole (stage)'d wooden s as piled

scream "there" small broken heads a dead

punch holes (stage) 'swood a dust dirt

punch't hole (stage)'d wooden s as

piled shout "target" flat head again

walled't's andscream "there" small

broken heads a dead

punch

holes (stage)'s wood

a dust dirt

shout "target" flat head again

walled't's and punch't hole (stage)'d

wooden s as piled scream "there" small broken

heads a dead punch't

hole (stage)'d wooden s as piled

scream "there" punch holes

(stage)'s wood a dust dirt

small

broken

heads a dead

shout "target" flat

head

again

walled't's

treble one

 or sing "bugs" each one

between one cracks again so wall far

saying "small" ones each step up a

ways another ceiling said "bugs" small ones

tune tap

s

grass fed say "it" sent to die

step s bargainss s none a alive

broke door said "it" can't won't will

let's canvas two the toes singing "it"

since say "divine" in yesterday s shake

the bag sing "again" as happened it

before scraping raw knuckles there and shake

"isn't" sung as dead buried with it

space money

pails then between corner at

is colder s steel sing "surface" in

deep'ss formed hollow say "sub"'s at then

it (pale) abstract then said "slime"'f in

technique (3) charge a against trust care

says "gone" send't finger back load un

singing "gone" working plans no (4) can

color up one corner twice said "care"

turnkey s deal'd sighing "'haustion" exhale all

burned finger a tip a stone singing

"after" sorrows then after association burn s

hole sets utter "that" over it rolling

tug tug tug sing it "tug tug's"

it up toothbrush over brush brush out

say "straps"'s between'd tug tug ever undo

tug where knee side said "pocket" do

Rex gets up from the table a

the couch is green in the living

room the picture on the wall is

the sawtooth's Rex turns to the window

the jet

skis stopped working and Tod

kicked a stump and broke his toe

Tod said "ow" a good never word

keeps better windy bitter's putt putt putt

specks cotton said "stringy" mozzarella balls as

flying 'round dug sing "in" deeps counter

top wipes' bell ring in sound'd agrees

say "chew" slow no smoker wrap up

buckwheat floor spread't singing "crushed"

acorn rising smells up 'fluence "Bob" say actions said "sickness"

'y grains die died saying "gone" myth a other times still

that'll that shout "out" repeat close makes

center (hall)'s flowing singing "out" but torn

a.m. swim says "out" that devil that's

satan : back it up throw it

back truck there are dump said "less"

horizontal flat press steel sing "but" the

thin cause tiny cracks pour "plus" pain

surface grayed't saying "not" that's or wheels

pick

to pick (3) said "call" t

break more of the same clean up

bony sing "little" piece brush'd miss any

more leaves or pick burrow deep r

bend checks face "too" left'd down dirt

eyes sing "bulging" belt'd up scalps ex

'hale again said "ooz" light brush dirt

left ears left saying "been" skinny less

year t a (e) nose snort "and"

months in which (f) taken wind's 's

away it a coughing "blink" drip t

a bigger snorts "now" t a e

clat r the pace shout "go" k

shits deep r singing "there" baby a's

unit s 'tached'd say "go" as k

drop't random d floor as once there's

grays half fell a boot up stepping

hands rails yelling "what?" shake it step

up a sense tell "again" hands wave

there dead 'spute s singing "what?" m

once fluid

u s say "bleak" sands

flat in groove sing "driersss" there blow

now granular is cubic's dare as torture

bending melts said "bleaker" flows pour'd d

sums four direction sing "touching" with mean

'ng holes chest say "me" when drops

finger (that foggy) vein fours read said

"touch" gurgle time s said "you" ok

has relation no one s say "bridge"

a linear no and said "arbitrary" push

pull 'over specks of spread's knife like

variable size hey "that's" initial s abuse

one s say "bridge" has relation no

said "arbitrary" push a linear no and

spread's knife like pull 'over specks of

initial s abuse hey "that's" variable size

said "arbitrary" push

spread's knife like one s say "bridge"

hey "that's" initial s abuse

has relation no variable size

a linear no and pull 'over specks of

depress't t says "thrust" and plunge'd a

run more at moment to sing "evade"

capacities and saying "duck" to compress avoid

scream "running" the moments before done t

make dream a step away saying "g's"

reddish t spins t playing "d's" for

board paints and nails through ever m

lose't out from't air that smells "a's"

weather d (ail) theory said "points" s

where tidal and it pulls pulls here

less one foot so "yes" bloody s

finger ass out peeled as opposed to

explosion each scream "six" 6 seconds of

walk and ways twist t a p

d whisper "7" six playing soft and

low spread margarine fog s inch s

done it yes

"once" jump off it

aren't air and sing "float"'d y it

retch a back up open eye'ee with it

ticking and bump (2)'d flares lit it

wood slated shingle sing "hang" doors pour

hole open wouldn't say "stop" escape t

two-part by anchored high long seascape s

red (pale) off cheek said "a" beaches

Rex stood at the window

one car one thought a car

Rex thoughts

at the Rex stood one car

window thought a car

one

blow t (p) tense say "are" t

concerning there was spread ground too t

and recent said "are" there or a t

slapping wind thirty knots less rope t

paste once new falter base more say

"has" return once new falter one place

says "it" flip it hand crosses teeth

flying sing "ever" morning runaway is runs

Rex thoughts

Rex turned to the door

mail below the slot

Rex sighed channel s around s around t frequent close hole

as judge as all t halts s

periods full cover magazine can

t s disappear dusty as wet s t and channel

s t frequent close hole as judge t halt s full cover

magazine can t s disappear as wet s t and channel t

chann t fr cho e as jusge t ht s ful cove mag ine cat s disappear

as we ts ta.

the task

Rex smells fried bacon from the morning

Rex sees headlights

Rex sits on the couch drools more

Rex is hot tired

have as wheeled a out gurneys line

times 8 (2) - ball foot s sing "got" one more channel inky deep

say "none" whispers pillow great full less

pedals so faster and fast all ply

quiet says "what" brushing friction so fast

brown splashes spoke "when" then spin fast

t careen to the overs s t

object to a tendency as said "long"

stable it a material vents a singing

"destructions" y e q here an

inherent ball forward balls back pinned in

chicken paralysis't 'nother trains load em up

say "binge" player lose guide on t

returning better two fixture two pour s

sing "on" tender where lessons are done

Rex's foot

is numb again push't

Rex can't remember

Rex gets up listens to some sound

Rex hears

Rex knows want in betweens

Rex can't speak it

Stan walks in step a step

Rex gets up't

instance'd strain stray gait saying "life" centers

stepped back into (barrel) lean't and second

sing "as" metal handle pulls short step

way from leave instance'dd phrase'd low r

bending in distinct chatter "ter" b h

m u spectrum never there above one

two singing "car" did they not belt

done swimming a walk or salve

bull tight full inch and foot say "ride"t

red effort blowing fuse knees say "ride"

it once tumbled across tapes around d

play minutes sing "ride"s cinch more up

m c i o shoved

against couch

singing "anti" insect spraying s f just

just got a message (5:) six h

wills was saying "fungal" to last n

mention at this said "cut" away tract

abel's left with arms bent left cross

singing "baby" plays all supple't as crack's

till then mumbles "cut" says note it

Stan stops moving at all

Rex doesn't move

Rex and Stan

eyes together

Stan sees Rex

Rex moves a foot to Stan

Rex stops

find a one 'psest under a bed

room say "fanned" low frequency (blue)'s where

all passing singing "fast" just pack d

where say "pill" roller over and it

Rex waits

smelly grass

Stan waits

text a jots as can well say

"do" pairs songs s are not a

paired sing "come" gets very specific p

just a reminder a need to scrap

Rex thinks rocks

there on

Stan's head

strike like well "similar" at it again

taken singing "nets" pedal't o means

holes bets 2 a tree knee down

away loses 3 a well "alike" to

slots everyone can get say "go" since

park it once often profit s all

backwards "go" said and harness gray for

line tugs knuckle pull hard sing "go"

beat regular people says "lather" yet it

the said "get" while it s for

pancake day today to tongue work a

harder match yell "basket" get a basket

controlling

alonging t shout "fuck't's" scratch it

throats less singing "fuck't" belonging burn it

arteries burn whenever caused by one more

paper towels more received yell "do"'s compress

blend pasted carve sing "rings" pumps slow

jealous but pour x place blank s

say "thin" mirage once meaning t and

fall or fall haven't screamed "gone" as slurp

buckle all friends (bail) treat s lacquer

a say "one" illness sees one other

frog s bag bug 'blin centered pieces

up to look s sing "one" s

Rex saw the clock

one wall

Stan heard

nibbled toe 'article pressure say "fans" bolt

on twist faster nails spin it fast

a chew around't said "pop" spin bolt's

can ups leg high r get away

Rex rubbed

a bone

Stan turned

the commitment to mature say "to" real

yet dead psychic 'bjects world distance goes

material sings "raw" gets 'usings exactly right

waits one interest 'more lost n wrong

Rex gets up walks

Stan

Stan just

a

Rex breathes

Rex stays

Quiet

Stan opens the utensil drawer

Stan says look

a cat

Rex looks

blade and cheese pizza singing "ahhh" gravel

chip can with small spray s real

handles form the shape that is

work sings "ahhhhhh" packet boat s t

close by

for task pass for say

"bread" code affect one close becomes shore

close sing "butter" which if (air) all

based off less feeble as exit burst

batter up s and sings "for" take

at narrow holes smaller lined sight than

say "trench" or similar dig (eh) would

because it mentions "that" instead stir d

turns massive in a clench say "five"

deal sing "hats" place as best between

and but under it a then said

"run" tamper pat it get to down

pinch't back s'gain hey "there" just a

speak "slowly" in the reads finger can

as'r verse "tell" u a a late

and direct grab motion singing "patch" less

Rex thought

Kierkegaard ate my doggy"

Stan's up

Stan walks

over

Rex waits

fence on position says "feed" one crow

peanut (call) more at waters over the

fence tails singing "then" spray it all

said "leave" g j goes there lone

triggers little s (bay) singing "ground" never'd

present s (d) say "in" it r

does place shades set yellowish u red

once said "the" fingering goes away pay

bruising that clears been sweep what much

getting said "prop" the steps in down't

worse with pulling wood bark plural hold

base s'break say "prop" it sing "prop"

quality meat quality grape mouthing "ah" mountain

s terms are a lot of a

say "blot" slow pushing boards up lean

in additions backwards a forward to g

Stan

Rex

face out

did what

a gallon blew "use" could

feel "5" track'd loss transparent grade saw

did adopt 'tation pulling singing "low" chance

feel't spew tiny big amount spreading g

Stan sings "oh, Andy

why does your head look like a potato?" FZ

Rex doesn't

free hand s charge tuck say "gaa"

yet another one that has a very

burning effect in the eyes s s

slow down to sing "gaaa" t o

tubes crimp't then have to can it

upper leg sing "inside" pull't levels branch

track tracks beg "it" 'ragged't drug thin

skins blood tacks on the pavement save

Stan presses

the oven button

Rex looks

drip 'ing'g

pray "it" should keep but

pray keeps falling away but saying "it"

dripping't g bait back read less but

pray'nn better a trig'tr will get it

meets tap rubbing down against edge s

meet knock caress up sing "6" s

meeting tapping rub down zero ball s

meter beep say "3" chase it says

Stan pulls

the cookies out

Rex smells

Stan thinks

it's a variable

Rex waits

ex lines victim sit home says "ply"

a couple years't some says "dose" it

softs clay like sing "has" gone hard

way n coal s brought solid e

write (one)

 "so what" 'iter (wade)

pushing (t) alive (eat) "bark, bark, bark"

break "say, it's young" young (er)

less (blood) pump (d) leak'd over

'rrr'nnnnnnnnn'nnn" step foot run

except once #22 soft says "bent" element

though never ore (iron) section mix say

"over" if a bunch or group's

-(N) can singing "clear" eyes pop open

referenced dead no helium says "the" wagon

mould't once tincture less pour said "the"

good peaks (e) silvery s up to

vast area from zero () out said

Rex looks

out one window

it as is any Stan

a territory two hands a country

a blend comfort island sing "punctuate" big

a spread s a g u

a out saying "/" slapping it a

pale

one pets another's song sing "this"

began while 20 mph saying "wsssk" k

eye drip less a rib if very

says "chair" s name one of those

Stan

Rex thinks

there yet?

Stan, no

trap gas hiss'sss blanket a out for

s calling "does" answer trick question there

less memory saying "it" some dig brought

than ask "forgive" write an up line'd

mock volume and () tuck's behavior need

a bug two grout climb't down over

smelling () o () singing "hah"

heap's drag even with three or four

Rex got

one did it

Stan pulls

gun wound

 'nt the scream "fuck!" 'no

just cause batter as ducks lanes wound

around scream "fuck!" very deeper't to blood

their 'ing never to be seen

Rex can

see the corner

Stan

can (not) cut a slow line say

"curl" pregnant worth edgy entropic bubble bath

singing "curl" splash't blood swirl future't bucket

another say "head" trucks ride by

Stan hallucinating

an anagram

Rex smacks

drug plug't say "s" pinch d

a less sentence a less sentence a

singing "t" played skip't over under response

zero chance to catch debt a skip

Rex licks

his lip again

Stan leans

+ hugs bale duo play just cancel

no more than a month ago saying

"belts" even start'd widen 'ning play say

"belts'" - carrots celery onions cilantro pintos

soon s to a b lever c

say "g" made several over to breaks

out sing "f" b as a as

the craggy hill e d c rolls

end v end a good match each

said "get" some regard s o people

end and belt "sum" over c e

or dropped't wings power it a down

impacts may (r)'s h jack't rush m

says "poke" two tongues lips back m

up so early sing "do" do do

and tow (s)'d slips splash up downs

bigger

zoo magnet zeroes (in) say "heavy"

forgot to a g r pulling

in suck dummy weeds sung "butter" flow

't ing 'thus may be floating around

Rex gets

up and stretche s

Stan (s) attitude

did well tell "braced" that history's bend'd

says "hard" going around dig deeper no access't sleeve sauce

bore off (e) clues

with less or less sing "deep" barber

Stan says

start the potatoes

Rex says, no,

Stan turns

to the onion

Rex looks

pairs are not available for purchase on

singing "dance" hey nineteen let the hey

scream "ahhhhhhhh" makes both human beings pairsss

for each character blend say "dance" heys

token

and say "about" ? j d

k less buck deep bottom s flow

bridge v 'ottom outa kcuby's sell q

pass set does'o saying "a" to m

Rex sees

potatoes swirl around

Stan stabs's'm'

Rex yells

"You betcha!" keep

Stan's hands

triples says "mint" mole viewed h

o f pecks 'round said "red" pimply

d i lip j s on

turn downs' double'd sing "figs" t p

Stan threw

up his hands

Rex wretched

pick it at it saying "gum" f

chew't been very a yell "drop" for

ever thing tiny b d holes do

bleeding wipe pinky awake sigh "es" por

Rex at

the screen looks

Stan can't

confuse r u y shout "birds"

no text less a a b

to crowd (field crows) bell top with

be turning on a ba field old'son

~ b and catch stairs'p gun –

~ d or practice fall againing'g –

~ c and drop say "pale" skin –

~ that traps boot singing "ahh" –

mumble "talk" p n t o a

h anyone can watch't s floor in

mumbles "over" s t i s nt

day or cook grain as a placemented

Stan pulls

a bloody body

Rex downstairs

Rex bites

down hard and

Stan's arm

=,\ "don't"

cram of holes bubble t

once technique s fr g jags there

=,\ "do" force 'ontal grabs push t

three is n t well not n

once technique s fr g jags there

three is n t well not n

=,\ "don't" cram of holes bubble t

=,\ "do" force 'ontal grabs push t

Rex thinks

it's getting cold

Stan stops

Rex pulls

the body along

Stan pushes

Rex noticed

streetlights off

Stan knows

trade r say "days" week or maybe

one more month that's (egg) sing "of"

more horizontal s breath "a" fail in

turds roll flat on around't s face

a sentence

(nake) g t i

copper sing "gold" 8 will s h

coin before two feet stomp "down" if

spin (burn'em) t four to land d

Stan throws

the bag over

Rex watches

Rex watches

Gale top stairs eye

Stan trash

plant b a s q's veil same

heap (balance)'d work all allow mass

of 'ron oat'd b x y sings "green"

rotted g i b's any carbon e

Gale says

"dump it there" there

Rex looks up

singing "blahs" parts 'icle in't j shoe

keeper where are the other (h) laces

tie t t a pole s k

say "blahss" yets's ever shape shape

dance

but d fi balance b just

all 'rty them say "bulletin" watch out

tech' s break one crush d after

esque t bray "knew!" it could spin t

Stan says

trash there to

Rex shrugged'd

crook't plagueish meat dish u l l

say "gaaan" broke (tv) splash ng out

a doors are a late s j

about said "none" tire drug'd blank smells

Rex drops

a knife again

Stan pulls

tension related as only brace with singing

"bells" are a t d a part

tied nickel wise's saying "ging't" end at

with relax u d a r t's

Stan sees

bright yellow lights

Rex's shoulder

exhale

over't with breath say "o" drp'

d k e and in lungs as

said "s" b x t are ruse'd

look v r a up u

one moment f d too long j

bark "aw!" shingled tuck'd backs put roof

four or could be sing "owww"'s 'n

really do zero as h i p

Stan gets

the shovel it

Rex digs

Rex can't

see that well

Stan knows

Gale digs

and digs and

Rex stands

carpeting g g (garde) screams "shitss" s

break up s g tail'g vibrating sings

"does" e m depending (g) sands j

y eah barfit' taken'd strip bares u

Sam barked

up the street

Carol stopped

'bounding g r say "bring" and bags

a 'trance a will t gone –

sing "grade" no alley or pressure b

going s isn't or blind't k nextdoor

Gloria steps

out on the porch

Greg squints

Gloria smells

bbq in the air

Glenn thinks

pain in't bulges say "dear" belted tight

[OBJ]pick pick pick at't grow'd late night

singing "then" [OBJ]once drop lesson in a

painted yellow to make orange as red

growth out our r or more say

"day" shirt up p put a pear

and tables't fun as a s to

singing "light" off bare le o apples

Glenn runs

missing a turn

Gloria screams

change change change pocket size to fit

sing "balls" a roll o vr t

stick and waits (2-) hour between work

sing "of" change change t y fires

rope 17,20

change change change pocket size to fit

sing "balls" a roll o vr t

stick and waits (2-) hour between work

sing "of" change change t y fires

bucket more (to) run h qua non

says "peckit" peel t spill against days

displayed spittle v a t s brought

said "up" drain o in o front

Gloria runs

faster and faster

Glenn stops

text b

as y say "speak" doesn't

'mitted traps boot not roll'd over rubbers

said "for" some f a say "j"

click r two soles'd sneakers they squeak

Glenn slowly

stops then stops

Gloria stops

Glenn stares

and stands and

Gloria stares

purple streak s f a cool in

a singing "shall't" spin spin a all's

streak f cool a s 'ish in

shot down r c said "weep" all't

plex for saying "truck" jumps off tail

s y i guarded's head p initiated

said "rides" plot s h and all

expect d c but over a whelm

Gloria stares

and stands and

Glenn sits

Rex pulls

the blanket over

Stan lifts the body

tuck'ed dagger t a great little b

and singing "'xposure" back s behind er

baking more than anything bell pepper zzz

again shouting "none" play off a this's

Rex sets

the body in the hole

Stan cries ahh

Gale stood

no saints here

Stan

Stan looks

up and says what?

Gale stands

Stan looks

again at Gale

Rex taps

miracle'd p b j's created buggy

sing "eggplant" chops's for the next times

forty plus d t said "tomato" hairy

standing backs grate garlic y c got

eclipse

say "buddy..." scatter u there was

pale or pale s left floor rub

knee elbow car top singing "mom!" g

asphalt a arm's stretch as skin burn

singing "birds" in the middle g sound

d place there circle d as gross

saying "land" bares c mistakes plays land

one street to n favor a forget

press t bays't 8 or singing "bella"

tucked inners 'rest seam r g bag

say "bella" 'enos lined through out down

s u scratch yet (bare) st up

Stan again

looks at Gale

Rex waits

bullet y ing traps scream "baaa" forks

left spoon rights ! but slow cook

ooze s 90 time s charge to

say "ennn o" plaster chipping away at d

'trac d

vat h one pillar crawl

downward bark cracks barkr' b and singing

"drug" tinsel s early r gas but

flaming o say "precious" pays h yet

Gloria then

walks down the street

Glenn follows'd

recognize y a great saying "from" to

see t is trigger d blood s

say "there" isn't a any more than

grasp't belt 'lief grazed when g fell

Gloria can

see the park lights

Glenn fingers

late dig v t over itch d

hang 'ging hang say "since" baser

'er softer dirt nearby s hum "m"

ers's m's h take w a t

Glenn walks

up along the side walk

Gloria point s

dragg'd off

o pens saying "five" o

tumble n roll o ver pitch a

finger o singing "just" sorries and more o

'man s break pulling o nly long'a

Glenn can

eat anything around

Gloria wants a donut

Gloria opens

the gate to Marks

Glenn scuffs

Rex tamps

the dirt down

Stan

Stan sits

down two buttocks sat

Rex

puncture wounding drips't can also a box

chew bubble up's screaming "no" table fingers

chop chop chop nails say "two" or

splashed floors splash outs a square table't

Marks is

dark and closed

Glenn stares ahead

Gloria likes

good beer and potatoes

Glenn sits down

Stan hugs

Rex on the stairs

Gale tamps

that no pull saying "bells" not where

just two pay d h yesterday j

s sing "who" dropper a saw in

'ing chairs back little pressure a f

Glenn sees

a liquor store

Gloria follows

tile grout bolts around flooring sing "garnish"

pepper t and salt faux (4) h

say "it" polish d that 'ythmic voice

raise glasses take a 'eye'd sore.

'nnection going

scream "oormall" bless a page

before because v o t sing "allll"

question a s and 'de in concrete

collapse b a see and where kill

pickle salad potato mayo singing "barbara" blues

ceiling't base on any other g turns

said "anne" forget'd vat s growth play

save't juggle spoon around h had's platter

Gale, Rex

and Stan holding each other

two steps

pick'k over't plan d tie quarter s

picker among singing "play" s hats n

hair y up s planets move't lesser

said "as" can 'ordinate where and ten

Gloria eats

potato/fish n drinks beer

Glenn licks

organ s play sing "baaa" baa crater

out steely debris's enter out's crawl out

said "bury't" heart s h left saying

"b" key s f c d hams

passage

'age 'ge 'e screaming "stop" all

every leg n arm's 'cuts over all

dying said "stop" tuck below'd

passage rolling g over on h hell

every leg n arm's 'cuts over all

passage 'age 'ge 'e screaming "stop" all

passage rolling g over on h hell

dying said "stop" tuck below'd

Glenn gets

down breathing deeply deep

Gloria get

Glenn eats

finger and a fork

Gloria rests

Gloria can't see her plate

Glenn can

dying said "stop" tuck below'd

passage 'age 'ge 'e screaming "stop" all

passage rolling g over on h hell

every leg n arm's 'cuts over all

dying said "stop" tuck s over to

below'd 'age

'ge 'e leave screaming "stop"

'sage rolling g on hells 'ort head

leg n arm's 'cuts over all dying

below'd 'age 'ge 'e leave screaming "stop"

'ort heads 'sage's rolling dying said "fall"

g on "stop" tuck leg'n arm's hellover

all dying 'cuts s over to spaces

Glenn eats

slowly chew chew

Gloria sleeps

cows pasture y bucolic c shit piled'd

chicken peck'r's many ground't saying "shat" and

bubbling over boils water feathers fly axes

fall deeper labyrinth stirred sing "soup" du jour

Gloria wakes

up fork spoons

Glenn's hand

spark sparkling spark'r's sing "blow" more dead

bodies more dead bodies shoved el'd b

e more dead't bodied's s shove ing

screaming "more" dead'd g body j more's

more dead

spark sparkling bodies more dead bodies e more spark'r's sing

"blows" screaming

"more" dead't bodied's s dead'd g body

j more's shoved el'd b shove ing

Gale holds Rex

arms over arm as

Stan sits

capture d a long pace'd bought d

left 'ing round punctua tion p after today

s saying "bald" growing't lace t before

here says "go" parrot't go over it

worse 'pearance h whenever a press r

head wounding saying "please" 'ness m soil

each rock j s t sitting less

said "less" more like a dead fishery

Rex plays

dead after roll

Stan scratched

Gale holds

the spatula one egg

Rex toss's

Stan walks

back out front from

Gale adding egg

tongue'a has x is n't lick

train't g j t d may

singing "crying" n i severed'g leggings bat

'ter colon esque'd say "cried" toes up

bends tuck'd b ack knot s where

end s smears 6 yester day singing

"places" bits familiar ly saying "it" here

back 'ard g t deals over all

Stan slices

a piece of the thighs

Gale waits

Gale looks

back at the door

Rex looks

pat it'd another pocket down kept buried

deep inside singing "slay"'s 'em rip artery s

filet 'es grip 'in't pole stair d when

saying "kill" bets up't sixteen to one

John

just stood outside and squinted

Sandra could see the front door

Sandra was thinking about her Selectric typewriter

"Oh, man..."

The Selectric sank. John stood on the stoop

and looked at the door

Sandra spoke three words then stopped

five words later John turn(s) his eyes to the street.

Sandra, then reached... the door knob

Sandra asked John, "tea?"

John asked, "hot?"

Sandra said ,"no, why?"

John looked at his watch

The tea service is silver plate

[dark music]

Sandra said, "soon it will be iced tea."

[jazz music playing]

Sandra laughed

[whistling wind]

John listened

"the whistling wind blows..." Sandra sang

John started to dance

[disquieting music]

John turned

Sandra stopped dancing

She picked up the knife

Mark stepped into

the room

Sandra buried the

knife into Mark's chest

paste r t y pick's scabb't that

break to breaks g another o that

sings "birds" speak "fly" into m o

walls necks broke reflect'd back in out

Gloria back

hand scrapes hands then

Glenn went

probe't where say "holes" some is more

e f later for away s e

months month sing "barrel"'t press hard r

creased table top cross tilt's an in

news b put say "death" death dug

stones up more bones 'ayered last bury

d sing "let"'s b 'tery are cuts

wrap t pushed over t till going

Glenn vomits

on the sidewalk

Gloria jumps

Gloria cuts

knife inner thigh artery

Glenn vomits again

inches an acres t whole place t

singing "some" tune pick't a again a

feet shuffle area with it in t

beg "more" tense spread across the field

Rex sits

on the back stairs

Stan isn't

bleak y er's raise low r again

extract'd push concave n bulge t again

singing "special" s fails s fail again

an a wall over say "help" stops

door creaks open tag back to it

[latin dance music] scrape floor ing t

[pensive music playing] tear parts g t borer

[singing] tag back to it ever less

force

take a book sing "not" always

a 'ority palms down'd pre-drugs full held

move leg break s t compound all

forward drag'ing leg ankle scream "no" m

Gloria [sniffles]

[flies buzz]

Glenn gets up

[dogs bark in the distance] pin it a

[dogs bark into the distance] touch it a

[dogs bark into the distance] carve it a

[dogs bark into a distance] pre sen t a

Glenn walks

away a sidewalk way

Gloria follows

Gloria sees

red flashing lights on

Glenn dives

interval s one up sing "over" dancing

high r stepping calf a toe j

interval t two g singing "it" s

lower u bracing rain s a through

[grave music]

hats flooring and sat in

say "gone" [slow tapping] dragging with where

[loud tap] singing "blue" s when there

to [knocking] over n then why s

Gloria's mind

isn't giving back and

Glenn won't help

trap d beg'ss s ladder t corner

d say "note" a t break t

just circular circ u l ar or

saying "um" thump in time all signals

Glenn sits

up and blinks blinks

Gloria's ankle

judge [wind howling] say "get" up bore

allow d f ing death y hole

s [snow blow] j l slushy singing

"the" other doubt r p l y

Rex takes

the trash out back

Stan drinks tea

say "oh"

bake it rise flake t

an a tension a belt pull t

sing "oh oh" flatten spoon spread t

tomato spread t cheese basil as t

Stan turns

on his seat away

Rex drops t

what says "beached" varied logs pile where

singing "across" two doors t f old

ringer bangs bang t late night s

where sing "gotta" go o to o

[stammering] better tracks b j i

[audience laughter] sets two in twenty two

[audience laughter] have mirror s d k

[audience murmur] sing "bar" and a good

Stan says

"Rex don't do that."

Gale listens

Sandra slept

till 6am

Rex

over bridge edge s pull it down

say "days" going g y e ball

d structure but sing "night" ly j

s stream o t flow k t

choose [car knock] says "tight" ly won't

feed s one box't [audience laughter] does

chose n sing "errr" baby scraps will

food [quiet birds] plugging it all up

[gentle instrumental music] crapper set sets in

[soft music plays] say "oh" smell that

waft d next doors [music] reach block

cry "man" arm it sever knuckle then

plague [soft oboe music playing] ring ing

[laughs] t r q p drop s

says "next" varys s clay [low strings]

bubble ups red yellows white drips s

Rex turned

the towel tightly

Stan gurgled

Stan died

on the floor

Rex went for the shovel

[soft instrumental music playing] y b c

[distant bombing] one light heads turned over

[scoffs] sing "steal't" pull d off thrown

[sniffs] say "does" b y c train

Rex digs

in the backyard again

Gloria and Glenn

[vocalizes] sent up saying "five" drag't round

[beeps] sing "mama" only 1 go 'er

[rooster crows] left at north right at

[sighs] saying "only" brick walls cement in

[ominous music] sing "guards" next force d

[silence] gun out shield d t where

torture common wound ing sings "t" over

and over [chattering birds] says "pull" in

Rex comes

in and stabs Gloria

Glenn screams

Fred runs

in tail wagging bang bang

Rex smiles

Rex goes out

side with the shovel

Glenn screams

period s take lever using say "write"

wait s pull pulled incite sing "reads"

three memory s side or side d

singing "tear" t a part as four

foggy say "shoot" s upset action d

under one rock [stressful music] green red

count s singing "emmmm" drop'd c bats

in [water drips] ear belief ? grow

[tinkling sounds] h v o p n

[car idling] v sing "7" p o

[scoffs] j m w a terrain is p

[wind whistles] says "9" there o oh

Rex turns

and swings the shovel

Glenn's head falls

Fred runs

jumping and rolling

Rex falls

Fred looks

up and sees something in the dark

Rex gets up

Fred runs

fast into the woods

Rex chases

[wind whispering] [line ringing] 5.2 [dog barking

in the distance] bits's just er'd another

[stammers] [grunts] [hooting] say "get" your butt

r n o z est't here press't

d o a t assist say "bug"

s y p in grasping't plunge in

splash'd sing "oh" hand in curve out

cutting v u s single said "sss"

[indistinct distant chatter]

bottle sing "few" paste

does hair gray [recorded whale sounds] in

barge s h s for say "variable" bounce

[coughs] t r a n could h's

[bottle clatters] b k p up is

said "don't it" usage a o e

coming down [rocks crashing] one is a favorite

singing "wrench" turn'p slang'd o p to

r shout [clacking sound] ideal to echo

say "group" s t r look down

granite wall [wheel screech] layer d the

ball'd bounce'd t r u fly halls

Sandra sliding

through the blood pounds the door

Glenn and Gene

Sandra hears

scratching on the ceiling

Glenn hugs Gene

to h f smackers

singing "bless'tt" chip'a

'way burrow in 'nr cable [drilling noise]

each bag filling say "more" b u

a let [noise] raise'r dive it 't

stub t stun s clip break off

say "bleat" [wind slashed trees] k pots

spill'd t singing "waving" off k on

speak "fog" g ba o toes s

[electric hissing] bells ringing during sex t

[barking dog] sniff 'round pale finger s

[music intensifies] hands downward nails asphalt d

[heavy breather] say "uh" [light zaps] bell

drops

to the floor and screams out

Glenn screaming

Rex drops

from the ceiling landing

Sandra stops

Ser•geant Barb

climbs

up the stairs

Glenn screams

[music fades] say "close" trunk [thunk] pole

[clattering] coins clat' r roller piss in

[clunk] from sing "not" a t pocket

hole s t y p key in

[sirens wail] b i a wall'd in

wall [echoing Bb's] ear plug'd s crossing

in blackout totals t say "go" glints

[clarineting] singing "lights" b o shine sine

de·tec·tive Judd

walks through the back gate

Ser•geant Barb steps in

second st. tunnels't [scoffed] wave h i

s windy saying "reach" t [synth horn]

rush r f s t r singing

"gravities" deeply embedded red sparkling acrylic wall

Ser•geant Barb steps

in a gun pulled pointed

de·tec·tive Judd

bald y

o not said "sssshhh" t

decord [soft strings] 'rible as pool s

pool 'round legs saw's d bone s

[square wave] buzzing u sing "sssshhhh" t

de·tec·tive Judd yells

come out back

Ser•geant Barb runs trips

ser•geant Barb lands

on Gloria head first

Glenn screams

a hear say "punchy" tenderly h o

p gurgle s o durable walls broke

sing "down" special ly no one a

a hearing beat d till dead'r o

de·tec·tive Judd ran

up the back stairs

Glenn screams

~

rake d gh j t dead ur

pressing harder't said "pregnant"

all un's earth grip'd ds j dry b crying

singing "tread"

keep on't biscuit s here

[sentimental music fades]

one t urn s

said "book" texture s

k uo now

[low hum] drops

pebble d by g p

singing "brass" s palm

rub't little p's

during the day

Ranger Ed would sit in his truck and watch highway 29. Nothing but dirt. Rocks and sticks sticking up out of the ground. Ed smoked. He used to chew but got lesions in his mouth. The sunrise is greenish with red highlights. The asphalt road became clearer.

no blues

no blues

nothing but dirt

no blues

he sat in his truck and watched highway 29

he used to chew but got lesions in his mouth

during the day Ranger Ed sat. Ed smoked

rocks and sticks sticking up out of the ground

the asphalt road became clearer

the sunrise is greenish with red highlights

[elevator thuds]

a bee landed on the

[speak indistinct] windshield. Ed blinked and

[computer trilling] looked. Glenn knocked on

[train whistle] the passenger side window.

Ranger Ed pulled out onto the highway, heading south. He

scoffed at a bee that flew nearby as he drove down the road

with determination. [scoffing]

[insect sounds]

As Ranger Ed navigated his way through traffic on the busy

highway, he encountered various sounds such as chirping insects

and clanging bells in addition to an occasional car horn blasting

loudly near him while driving.

He smoked Pall Malls.

[singing]

[bang]

Ranger Ed

winced with a dramatic sting playing into effect

within moments after pulling up onto this major

transportation artery connecting cities together by land

across long distances - one could feel tension

building rapidly from both drivers' perspectives

due their sudden maneuver.

Ed blinked, lit a cigarette.

Puff, puff. Sticks and rocks sticking up.

[band]

Ranger Ed pulled into Bob's Groc-Gas Mart.

Squinting. [music fades out] as he stepped

out of the car, the country music playing on the

radio followed him, casting a foreboding

shadow over the deserted parking lot. [droning noise] bees [loud

white noises] The morning air was heavy [music fades out] with

the smell of gasoline and [crunch crunch sound] burning oil,

making Ed's stomach churn [buzzing] as he walked towards the

convenience store.

Bob's Groc-Gas.

prints bit say "from" there back there

cry's nailed in rolling singing "water" s

real deals t g t done in

say "times" a jet stream h z's

the's print

of bit's [ticking sound]

that say "from" r located far's

behind s now, w continue roll't sing "trigger" 'bout power

water't deal'ss singing "parallel"

getting done't with determ' work (ing) [breathing]

scenes now we continue roll sing "about"

power't water'd deals indicat's activity far

t behind scenes singing "parallel" determin't drugged t

work prints bits create a ticking sound'r

'sman say "ridiculous" blue at horizon has

b m o picked since July later

singing "smoke" s august owls towers could

breach swim in v gathers till full

pints many singing "mary" (g) block steps

charg't p l 'ennies o m step'r

down one another twos' say "mother" may

more be c n p b r

[quiet ominous music]

 y lots tears k

[light music] t a song sung "very"

[nose singing] n a place it there

[light tense music] check check check t

the look [drone sound] bask rt t

b b broke say "uh" can bottle

box [sounds] break'd t a back and

this s g sing "rrrrrr" look a

one isn't b b broke saying "pregnant"

box and box s [wooden sounds] break'd

t m o back that s g

singing "gggggr" look't make'd as proof t

box a ox t [tap sounds] break'd

40 is v c burns sing "preee"

look'd make't as proof says "just" k

t m o back that f s

[water running sounds] be bp a l

under some house say "shock" in one

hallway run another hall way s singing

"shallow" bruise d [dripping sound] b t

Ranger Ed walks

into Bob's Groc-Gas-Mart scuffing, scuffs.

He steps just inside and burps. The music stops. Bob says "hi, Ranger Ed."

[ominous music, again]

Ranger Ed says "got any pizza pretzels?"

As Ranger Ed enters Bob's Groc-Gas-Mart, he scuffs his feet on the ground, creating an unintentional scuff. Stopping just inside the door he burps loudly, interrupting the music that was playing. Bob greets him with a hesitant 'hello, Ranger Ed'.

Inside Groc-Gas-Mart Peter stops playing the piano in the corner. Bob coughs and coughs. Peter is a stocker. Ranger Ed say "hey Bob." Cookies are on the first aisle, chips by the cold case near the beer. Pizza pretzels.

Inside Groc-Gas-Mart, Peter stops playing the piano in the corner. Bob coughs and coughs repeatedly as if trying to clear his throat while standing near the aisle containing snacks such as chips but not cookies...

Outside Bob's Groc-Gas-Mart through the back door, chickens [sheep bleating]. Ed was still constipated. "Dammit!" Codiene. "Hey, is there any Colace?" Bob stammers "yyess." Peter just

sat.

Peter coughs. Ranger Ed turns and walks out down a few steps. Bob coughs. And Ranger Ed walks muttering. He gets to his truck. The rooster vane on the roof points east. 7am. Saying "Dammit, where's my wallet?" [blowing wind] sands't [chuckles] Ranger Ed laughs turns and walks back. Climbs some steps, stops, "Bob, did I leave my wallet?" Peter coughs, sits down. Bob says, "I don't think so," coughing, "are you missing it?" [wind kicks up]

say "turning" t j as large as

r tracks long lines trail t sing

"rounds" turn'd out language in wards o

ur t package d perfect l y

Ranger Ed says "yeah, I think I left it here."

Bob leans over the counter and Peter holds the door open for Ranger Ed. Bob holds out Ranger Ed's wallet. "You want a cup a coffee?" Bob asks. Ranger Ed says, "naw, I'm good." Peter gets down on the floor and watches the ants. [sheep bleating] [owl hoots] Ranger Ed declares, 'I think I left my wallet right here!' as he points to the empty space on the table next to him. Bob slides over [scrapes] to him while Peter opens up two more chairs with one hand each before resuming their game involving cards they found lying nearby which was likely forgotten by

previous customers

[loud breathing] from many nights ago since no one remembers playing any games recently at all let alone leaving behind something so valuable after just having eaten dinner together only hours earlier than this moment happening now between these three men standing there silently staring [mouth breathing] blankly into thin air wondering what could have possibly happened [loud snores] during those few short minutes when nobody else seemed interested [hooting] enough even bother checking if anyone had pickedpocketed anything yet because surely someone would speak up [gggggg] otherwise right?

Scratching, Ranger Ed points frantically [screeching chair legs] to an empty spot on a cluttered table amidst cluttered screeching chairs squeaking [cello slashing] across tiled floors, [wind howling] the last remembered placing his leather-bound wallet before it vanished [howling wind] meanwhile, Peter meticulously [sniffing sounds] inspects every crevice of nearby discarded [banging shutters] cardboard boxes searching for any sign [slapping window dressings] indicative that someone might've taken advantage [chicken whistles] when distractions ran high amongst diners [shouting] in boisterous conversations post evening meal buffet. Chicken only.

scratching,

Ranger Ed

[screeching chair legs]

cluttered table amidst

[cello slashing] across tiled floors, [wind howling]

his leather-bound wallet vanished

[howling wind] meanwhile

Peter meticulously [sniffing sounds]

[banging shutters] cardboard boxes

sign [slapping window dressings]

someone might've

[chicken whistles] distractions

diners [shouting] boisterous meal

buffet

Ranger Ed

[screeching chair legs]

[cello slashing]

[wind howls]

[howling wind]

[sniffing sounds]

[banging shutters]

[slapping window dressings]

[chicken whistles]

distractions

[shouting]

[footsteps approaching] tap tap tap say "uh?" singing

"muhmuhmuh" 12 less exit s a

[footsteps receding] tap tap tap 'agments from

here there (3) spots t d out as

[song ends] Ranger Ed drives off, looks back to see Bob and

Peter waving

[pants]

checks's over sing "checkeredddd" s weight o

danger (ous) 4' s 5'd s s

say "pastsss" or emergency marked line s

o

little scrawl friend ly checkers one over

o

when wind blows't through

,2 [voice shaking] say

"bits" the installation by multiple

units not shape

t [low metal clank] tacked 27.2

end to forming lines

patterns across walls

ceilings floors windows

thin internal dot's t

each wire structures

slight movements soft

metallic sounds [wind blows wire]

similar heard

lightweight hollow

tubes cement'd

[slapping hard] another

Ranger Ed doesn't think or worry. Driving down to turn off left at

Lincoln Lane road. Emotional thoughts strangled. Guards shout.

Ranger Ed screeches, halting . "WHAT?"

[music fades] "MORNING RANGER ED!" Guard 1 said, "GOT YOUR

MESSAGE!"

[psychedelic music] Ranger Ed blinks rolls the window down,

"WHAT?"

dust envelopes all of them as

Ranger Ed stops (carry it over) division

h = g scream "inside" s change

nothing saying "out" v s an encampment

—[wheel spinning sound] sing "whirring"

as the dust settles, it becomes clear that Ranger Ed has stopped

division'd carrying

remnants

[people shouting in]

with Ranger Ed screams /inside//

say "changes" everything leave

said "grinding" [whoooooooroo]

what out s forming encampment

[pen scratched ing] sing "bows" j e

[keyboard clack clack] clack'd (3)'s kinds of

[floorboard creak] say "balls" v a named

[dog barking] and barks b g crashing

[ominous music] vocal chords fleur time floorboard creaked

saying "crinkle"

something vaguely resembling balls't dog barking

forces an ant farm waves against shores [swishing sounds]

[line ringing] 'ging temp ure s

[inner voice sound] 'one y pump r

[rings] buried play s back s

singing "ahhhhhh" t s [room echo] f

[crunching metal]

Ranger Ed battles

from the wreckage his face squinting pain's determination

singing "waaaaaaaaa"

[more crunching metal concrete] loose Ranger Ed stumbled

backwards falling heavily [heavy breathing] gasping despite'd

surg's

[unsetteling music stops] some's 'cross t where

[FOOTSTEPS] spark sputter'd singing "eyebrows" a tensor

say "bet" laugh r the points d

jangling [feetsteps] do (once) as one pattern

[chattering] uneasy settled over realized't ahead gambling

worldly [snorting] under singing "would" humor misfortune't

(or) higher converse [cough] mainly because there [chuckles]

Ranger Ed said "verse"regard potent have'd

stages pick't say "peeving" s a gain

0 matches [wind in pines] pipes bleed

coming prick't sing "ooooooohrr" chance't place t

g o space s around er in

[pulsing noise] break t g h a

[shattering glass] pulse't't frames a t s

pass say "on" sandy [scraping foots] but

singing "breaking" toast eggs b d exit

Ranger Ed gets up

dusts his hat high

critical frames't broken eggs s two dead

Guards a burning truck sing "blues" s

[distant screams] [distant yells] more crunchy gravel

spores't sang "gooooooorr" gated loose non s

spectral 'eral 'uclar drug'd 'n beg s

granual 'ly said "on't" s'condition days a s

bucket with't dug up hand rubbing as

bug vent d a bug singing "ccccccccc" more

[groaning sounds] no one around Ranger Ed

moved or y s q less

trades one says "ddddd" gets up it

Ranger Ed stretches out sand singing s "ssssssssssssss" keep

/fog/ j o open eyes

finger in [screaming winds] closing for

[crashing music stands] Ranger Ed reaches out

buried up say "when" s o table

chairs throw [percussive noise] across one's

chairs [crash noises] up sing "air"

more

d 'gainst Ranger Ed's legs up r

Ranger Ed Ranger Ed Ranger Ed where

once [whistles] singing "ohhhh" [stammers sighs] chronic

wound's heads thing s degree dead s

just [whistling] remember t h s next

ten/20 feet 'main s absolute and high

r sang "doodoodoo" 'alation c 'gee a

tipped's spikes say "borde" lines fence f

shirt barbs t pull't hit rock 'st

escape't park (rounds) said "pray" don't it

butts up 'tables s u o too grain

y too singing "high" level r 'arked

squeaky front tires's (rounddd) j e marble

[no audible dialogue] ambulance ranger Ed mesquite

blowing past say "balls" where's goes hs

[wheezing sounds] crack 'ing 'ing ps d

hour ps o find eyeball sing "roll"

now the ambulance [tire sounds] just r

Ranger Ed eyes wider screaming "waaaaaaaa" [chuckles]

but singing "dadadada dadada dada da duh"

d oxygen s in some siren d

Ranger Ed wakes

vomits door panels's van

top b t hats saying "where…" hands

there grabbing't riding gurney'd 'ceptiond doors next

f p slapping d hard er er

t l - much (asphalt) scraped out

say "look" between nail/flesh blood d r

broke n t and [bells ringing] saying

"there" s one syringe o tape d

[rushing water] c y gurgles reach t

[somber instrumental music] b w k without

[dog barking] stretch tendon t 'orns s

[coyote yips] singing "money" g m e

arms cross [strings building] b open'd up

[sighs] says "a spring night" pittosporum

s [cell phone rings] fix d (odor)

singing "oak leaves" [landing sounds] p t

[words gusting] nose up lips out'r up

[cars honks] cheese cheeses cheese s s

[barking seals whooshing waves] cheese cheeses cheese s s

"cheese" [bird tweets]

[birds singing outside]

drag roll ing hills

[whistlers] green y g ends of't sing

[birders whistle] "rrrrrrr" Ranger Ed sees dense

t burns as out [whisper] green wood

salts salts salts say "dried" tomatoe s

Ranger Ed sits up't jeez kangling c

once play s (berry) finger slide't s

salt salt singing "tongue" s grappling t

[tense music] name a y hat r

[tense music fades] named and yet say

[tense music] "oh 'alices" again but wheres'

[tense music fades] a hole's same s

[high pitched metal climbing] but melt d

[sighs] z'd dribble tubes'p suck back arms

singing "brazzz" [exhale] toes and nails each

r say "as'sssss" put f start car

[somber oboe playing] g r s a

[super futuristic music] j tw k o

[jazzy piano playing] v sh t a

[super futuristic music] c r gu o

fleas [violins]

grab coat s h cat

floods [low horn sounds] towel up roll

fall [cups hit floor] crash b r

winter [penny whistle tune] burn the fire

[mysterious music intensifies] now try trial triangle

d u a pits holes sing "waaaaas"

plays c y [mysterious music fades] with

baggy say "relax" t work poker verb

raise each (leg) r s once or

grate j say "hunger" h t ever

as sing "is" lower t h e

lower backer s let go non m

z yeah say "oh" [tinkling piano] bears

dance Ranger Ed wakes singing "ahhhhs" ripp't

sheet knee upper [some music] no safety

but rhythmic toe tapping just bust z

Detective Burger looked at Ranger Ed asked "what's your

name?" 1 j a tube

saying "name" tucked in [minor chord] fit

Ed mutters "eh" back in get out's

pucker the taste

hit Ranger Ed hard'r

[deep mechanical bumps] a foot floor't a

slapping t say "hey!" slide r y

g mouthing "rey" are k h ey

bees a sing "chaa" ch ch busy

the thing (walk) c f [deep hum]

bird whis'tl ht figure 'ing Ranger Ed

boxes out saying "once" logic the dogs

[noisy rocket engines] p drip r against

say "just" v x t d asleft [putt putt noises] fender bent in

sing "ones" pops in out r n

[door closes] over sand r bank s

sang "green" ry tiny (spot)'s gut response

Ranger Ed says "nothing" none s rrg

[clanging] head hand rs 'nate a ring

[squeaky wheel noise] not guilt a complexi'

ty bare floors's slipper photo'd b p

[horns honking] m d o shuffle buff

d water spray sing "just'a" smooth oak

pleads "mo"

after cent to face the

[crashing sounds] bells t f k pushing

[hard sole steps] says "no" dollars as

c g t 's que to p

[soft ominous music] go u t where

say "blinks" pat one another get it

where singing "blinking" tremors wrist twist up

[blowing winds] one circle s j o

craft hands rub d y p gut

pinch vale v ues' b opens k

[singing sound] says "breaks" prop d up

squeeze ur's yet [pops] drain o p

singing "all" d a rott d o

but one s more Ranger Ed walks

grabbed pole [pink noise] desks line similar

'oblit 'str as div'd a 'trary h

[tapping noises] drive drive er eyes up's

overtone fades [schschcshm] Ranger Ed does it

[breathes heavily] by hear tap glass look

say "hey" u h trip line face

linoleum d h t eye n d

[metal banging]

[sinister music]

[finger scratch]

[nail bites]

bend d has as s say "jokes"

saline r be [grating] engage reduce s

[sigh] sing "blues" t u g razor

pepper y lemon s o glues k

none f h intend exist t s

Detective Burger sits eye brow lift so

[chilling music] sugars crust 'ver t pole

is tray stand cotton blanket say "uh"

[rustling] plates rat ling't shout "wa" turn

g [crumbling] bricks blocks bury d

Ranger Ed falls [metal hits] screaming "wa" push

[screech] glass door roll lung'd dust sss

[tense music] say "that" since drips and

[chuckles] and [chuckles] eat paint r s

eat [crunch] and [crack] bucket left where

[screeching music] sing "that's" perfect ly diffident

Ranger Ed face

flat nd brew t

saying "there's" butt up's spring [grate sound]

one leg pull singing "oh, asphalt, yoko" come

n together a h u e tears

ask "does" a one involving s done

[soothing jazz music] keep falling 'gatively't somes

Ranger Ed eyes and open [tympani rolls]

as flutter'r a burn ng arms do

[weird ass music] bell touch't burn s

saying "eh" e h [clears throat] burning

once day less cut't [phone ring]

more coughs it f 'rning [loud coughing]

[uneasy music] pulls tummy up table top

singing "brother" a donut a knife a

[solo clarinet] say "good" icing an icing

and sprinkle s red blue green yellow

Ranger Ed rubs the crust say "ow"

eyes a finger [scraping sounds] Ed looks

says "bua" thinking steel [wheel rollings] a

cart no truck none t a s

[music stops abruptly]

hissing Detective Burger turn

d outside trucks [crunchy wheel] toes finger

says "obsess" t well if well that

[sighs] flighty blue shadow left eye t

do do sing "dah" do [tense music]

'pensive batches f t with as

fingers n ails sing "brush back" face

it [rubbing sounds] dah do dah do

fields hay say "one" scarecrow beat g

ground holes [loud dance music] scuffle g

singing "refuse" Detective Burger a and Ranger Ed eyes

screaming "Lavinia" s straw

handy waves [country western music] particle

dot saying "jot" down Detective Burger more

b i k e a first goth

[note bends] a couple back corner

down a hill a knife a cut

skin "ow" muscle "ow" bone through paper

towel [gate buzz] two heads say "titus"t

[static crackle] pies sing "ow"

Detective Burger works g it

some s change [booming] walking t silence

t sing "nothing" stumpy drag'd carve dirt

breaks Ranger Ed pulls p o up

eye slit [chugging] signs some say "maybe"

[alarm beep] it Detective Burger head over

[soft hum] tomorrow g o drug or

voice sing "sons" 'ora close door r

[breathing heavy] t r 'urninus drawings burn

Ranger Ed s wheel chair [violin music]

compart'd say "where" [quiet piano tinkle] desk

paper pen s h t o write

r sign r singing "yaa" [tinkle] s

a neck a neck a hand a

hand a neck a hand a hand

a neck a neck a neck a

hand a hand a neck a hand

one turn r say "box" clothes sing

"diaphragm" push rs Ranger Ed's hat

worn edge (from) sun light tobacco [sax

music] all off brush it jugs up

one barb to

[string noises] jerk d

back Detective Burger eyes Ranger Ed look

d up another barb's spat [baritone hum] 'tl

Detective Burger's winced's cheek say "aliens" mow

just button up [thudding] foot s step

before Detective Burger wince wipe say "there"

s [shrieks] Ranger Ed kick out leg

break [crush] Detective Burger falling inner thighs

[crash] Detective Burger roll s leg down

over a back singing "part" floors rack

t hands grab ng y [metal clank]

gloves blue t eye and say "parts"

peaches [bang] smashed sing "water" Ranger

Ed eyes s up [click here] hands

around necks s account one say "more"

dropped on sand deep [crunchy] no belt'd

Ranger Ed says "there" arms gone r

[quiet violas] landing yesterday f y causing

Detective Burger gurgles blood 3 creature dozen

leg v million light year s ago

clear a horizon

[soft drums] ch say "flows" bits sand y friction s blue r

singing "out" one drug two g tuxedo

s [softer drumming] 7/8 ||: four to three :||

o

Metal beast, teeth of steel, Treading amber waves, Midwest symphony, engine drone, Harvest hymn, the earth's soft moan. Rows and rows, lined like veins, Blood of land, gold in grains, Iron heart, methodical pulse, Hands of man, nature's pulse. Sky burns, late day flame, Dust motes dance in dying light, Cornstalk whispers, secrets shared, Beneath the hum of twilight's blight. Steel maw chews, relentless bite, Golden kernels, cascading flood, Stalks bow, reverent, to the might, Of the machine that drinks their blood. Wheels churn, earth's heartbeat, Harvest song, a rusted hymn, In fields where shadow's whispers meet, The tractor's hum, a sacred hymn. Sun sinks low, horizon's kiss, Metal fades to twilight's shroud, Corn collected, day's last bliss, Night falls, stars are plowed. chatgpt: Write an experimental poem about a tractor collecting corn… (where now do we go now's)

metal beast

treading amber

midwest symphony

harvest hymn the earth's

rows and rows lined

blood of land gold

iron heart methodical

hands of man nature's

sky burns late day

dust motes dance in dying light

cornstalk whispers secrets

beneath the hum of twilight's

steel maw chews relentless

bolden kernels cascading flood

stalks bow reverent

of the machine that drinks their

wheels churn earth's

harvest song a rusted

in fields where shadow's

the tractor's hum a sacred

sun sinks low horizon's

metal fades to twilight's

corn collected day's last

night falls

stars are plowed

(where now do we go now's)

,16 [saw whir] several tree + once top

r t say "think" y s tail

sing "bbbb" eight fox [lapping waves] bare

walk s t said "puzzle" d there

pull't a f pail water s trapped

g to half wade tidal s and

say "breezes" blow t [brrrr] tar mass

wash ng [whoooos] tick s crawl up

pretty less t h blue [oooosh] wade

g tidal say "biiir" water bath foamy

wind s [ooooshr] r sing "can't"

p k wavy o lift the arm

wind s [ooooshr] r sing "can't"

wash ng [whoooos] tick s crawl up

p k wavy o lift the arm

g tidal say "biiir" water bath foamy

say "breezes" blow t [brrrr] tar mass

pull't a f pail water s trapped

g to half wade tidal s and

pretty less t h blue [oooosh] wade

wash ng [whoooos]

tick s crawl up

p k wavy o lift the arm

say "breezes" blow t [brrrr] tar mass

wind s [oooshr] r sing "can't"

g tidal say "biiir" water bath foamy

g tidal say "biiir" water bath foamy

say "breezes" blow t [brrrr] tar mass

pull't a f pail water s trapped

pretty less t h blue [oooosh] wade

g to half wade tidal s and

pull't a f pail water s trapped

wind s [oooshr] r sing "can't"

g to half wade tidal s and

p k wavy o lift the arm

wash ng [whoooos] tick s crawl up

pretty less t h blue [oooosh] wade't

[suspenseful music] 6 uc t clef k

run time 35 sing "para" check d

[clanging] ee changes up curving into less

say "basket" basket [mellow jazz] spaces bass

box

small saying "letters" . ' s

[weeping sound] g e half facing s

[burning crackers] historically a bird s

[train whistle] a film grazing grass s

one task say "hell" of a b

second task sing "oh" mark it there

another task g u ether mask up

[hissing valve] shout "hell" as t changes

[wind howls] bowling each say "yes" but

one or tentacles between b c [paper

rattles] window slap s t sing "corner"

glass wood [weeeee] holes scream "aweee"

since once s [wet tires] wet handle

s say "trouble" occur d h r

once c [splitting woods] h sing "torn"

ranch hand one slips up h p

kept un d r [pound sounds] break

air s hot r n hot red

red r burst r s say "can't"

see some other s sing and "sawsss"

red r burst

r s say "can't"

kept un d r [pound sounds] break

see some other s sing and "sawsss"

s air n r hot red hot

again [birds chirping] t a an chase

singing "all of me" [crashing sounds] p

bell ring 'ing c i o wood

one branch [wind] slip a slip r

crow [rattle] sing "run" v o routes

bell ring 'ing c i o wood

singing "autumn leaves" [crashing sounds] p

again [birds chirping] t a an chase

one branch [wind] slip as two ers

f u t ar spins k up

[metallic sounds] v' b tail r 'gree

deep [panting] said "one" farther reign h

crapping [plop] s f 'very o m

grey block s at intervals t y

[laughter] say "sentence" as 1 test where

since other d s grow taller g

sing "syllable" s h h out there

"don't"

jump 'ings' one more druggy s

finger s concrete s rubs [voosh] r

nail scratch each deep wax r trace

says "the" watering milk flow that grate

a band ribbon say "stretch" j pull

s back forth [quiet bassoon melody] grapie'

a apple slice or [baby chicks chirp]

s pecks a slapping sing "bounce" 'ng

say "still" electric spit [shpsh] where on

g o l less r k t

[crispy burning] a leg out sing "in"

take an a rail a car

say "not" 'ing makes a point separation

b y gain r [wet licking sound]

'new sing "rights" spider jump p p

[crushing ice sound] bright lites big'r city

toe sock say "less" blood runny wave

t j t [drag] s a leg

singing "less" knock t over or it

[scrape] drugged s f carry bone

[indistinct murmur]

turn table f loose r

ask "did" [lip licking] j g chair

door [bang] say "it" adept d push

it [splash] farther mop s wide r

mix saying "pkss" bleat "nayyy" b outs

another page r d break s

save t sing "as" where there break

[squish sound] paper crease's v t mow

ix say "ps" leat "nawa" c out

anoth'r pg r ds bre' s

sa t sing "aps" wher ther brea'

['uish sound] per ease's t v mod

x sa "p" lea "nwa" cb ut

'ther pg t ys bgre" rk

a t sing "ap" wh th br'

['uis oun] er ese's g e mo

[alerting alarm]

a t sing "ap" wh th br'

['uis oun] er ese's g e mo

x sa "p" lea "nwa" cb ut

'ther pg t ys bgre" rk

[honk goose]

t a sung "verb" hr th bro'j

['is on] e e's f e co

p ya "o" seas "metonymy's" x it

'they pig d mumble "gray" rwk

[honk car]

a thing regarded as representative or symbolic

of something else, especially something abstract. "with a hammer."

"the ant colony has been portrayed." met·a·phor

thing regard [water running] g r symbolic

else sing "especially" 'stract say "with a

hammer" ants colon y hs bn portr'

aid met a por s fy splashed

[water running] g r

symbolic

ants colon y hs

say "with a

hammer"

aid met a

'stract thing regard

por s fy splash

bn portr'

else

sing "special"

[doors close]

The insect bite makes

Me scratch like a rabid dog

Itching ankle itch

The mosquitos go mad

When they see me coming home

Ranch style living it

Twelve bits grow too high

Draining worms to many grooves

Asphalt slowly drains steams up

[doors click open] s insect bite make't

scratch a rabid dog lick s say

"t" itchy ankle mosquito sing [sqeee] they

as coming bbq bk yr m ts

grow high red s turf e r

'aining slither bits say "pail"

to groove't punch out [sticky sound] ride't

s'phalt slow rain s steams s r

t bits r

row to high's

'raining rms two many reaching u hand

'phalt fast r rains stream s down

drive out g x or lowest t

[clamoring voice] to high r raining rms

two singing "blows" or lowest t down

[music playing] fast not r driven m

x g say "hand" bitter s

[console beeping] to say "blow" drive left

low t raining res x g say

"hand" [grunts softly] low f downward over

fast not r bitter say "er" s

[ssssssh] sing "liver" higher t snow r

in g said "tray" b e t

drive left over bump t [sighhhh]'s h

h sweet slower g j each foot

[bbbbbg] said "just" timber b sleet b

high h saying "bran" o u s

weep felt's b none inner d [gargle]'s p

o sour wedge f t wear d

[caaaaaa]

screaming "a" timbre v select d

dense k in mumbles "a" tickle toe

gave one s smell crack s [a]'f

s pale r sweeter r crack pull

test s d h yr b

test c f s nr e

test h m ce d a

test s d h yrt b

stamp s d h yr b

bake c f s nr e

yeast h m ce d a

muffin s d h yrt b

spin s d h yr b

the c f s nr e

bottle h m ce d a

again s d h yrt ;(t

[chirping] spin r water b f

the some [quiet whistle] pierce a n

t glasses g s say "well" '

trigger d there ;(j left s

Susan and Jim

walked out in the street. A smell of beef cooking and burning followed them into another alley. Jim's tavern though old and worn was a relief from the days. They walked in. Smoke, leather, gin and tonics in succession, a, a.

later the…

Buck walks in and finds a table for two next to a window. Jim flips burgers with his fingers. He mixes the coleslaw with his hands, mayo, a trash can in the walk-in.

Chet yells, "Ed, someone called and you need to go out to the river and see if your island is underwater." Ed mixes the coleslaw and thinks, "it's not an island if it's underwater."

Inside Susan finishes the accounting and sips her coffee. The place has four tables and a bunch of chairs. She waits to unlock the front door. There are two cars in the lot. Both red.

Buck has been sitting at the table and Susan doesn't notice him. She unlocks the door and switches the sign. Open. Susan asks, "coffee?" Buck nods.

a spider

hangs down the window. Susan lashes out with the Daily Post.
Buck ducks. Light music playing. Ambient sounds. A bl e o
"o hh Portia" n oo rains. Buck looks out the window.
The two cars leave. Susan takes Buck's order. Two eggs over
easy hash browns with lea and perrins on the side. Ed thinks
about the island, "no island, there," Ed says to the eggs staring
back and singing "think of me." Chet answers the phone,

"uh,uh."

Susan brings Buck's eggs and hash browns and the coffee pot.
Slow drip. Chet answers the phone and yells at Ed, "hey Ed, Fred
said your island is under water." Ed sips some coffee and puts
cheese on the burgers. Buttered buns.
pear [boom] g u ett where s
apple [boom] t a w sh t
corn [boom] c switch lower back forties
beet [ahhh] b i t sing "ahss"
peas [thud] grasp f t ing up
squash [thud] g place h k outs
melon [thud] crapper overflow s j flow
zucchini [thud] flowers o e fried butter

Chet went

out back to meet the delivery truck. Tripped over a brick. Face

first in the gravel. Shouting "fucking bad day." Jumping down,

Guy said, "hey!" Chet got up and laughing, "salad days, ya

know."

radish [high note] a bit'a taco left

potato [low note] scraps chopped lettuce is

cilantro [mid note] garlic black bean tomato

onion [notes] garlic chili chopped slow slow

z y r s a pack

[slicing sounds] divide s f r particle

less quarter saying "try" non e end

o [grinding sound'd] own b k cutting

Ed thinks,"so the kids are playing on a soccer field, fooled them, the

planes landed." Scoffs,

another order. Two eggs hash browns and canned peaches. Again,

"mainly through signing."

one block [crashing sound] g a w

s block [crashing sounds] could of broken

a block [crashing sound] veins blood'd a

again [crashing sound] fracture p nd d

stone falls

[blocks] break t p cs

say "belts" helm tk steerer r as

another dropping piece each sand each

s slow tumble [blocks] cause to a pc

ana [screaming male sounds] h o s

amor [yelling female sound] s r p

pho [barking dogs] h k r q

sis [honking horns] round eye glance s

a [breaking wood] view f h k u e

w [crunching wood] viewed h l a p o v

r [sawed wood] see n b k w d r sections t

y [sanded wood] seen under s d b i o

id [slicing sound] f cucumber stop it b k

is [grunting] t s q hat h i f

sent [quiet chopping] pops pop b u br

ed [yelling sounds] down down g k f'd

[door opens] click't d o y p

[door closed sound] slam't jump s out

[door opens] g e s upper edge

[door hangs squeaking] hang'd b e b

pic

[sounds of wind] h d out

kles [waves lapping] b x of out

eat [rocks falling] fy j c m

in [hand slaps] bt r ng s

foot [birds tweeting] h o w jt

print [birds tweet more] y w bo

book [tweeting] dull wind flap s t

shelf [tweet] one water no surface b

p h t d [oboe] pills it

s y w q [oboe] s scatter

q r o d [english horns] rousing "ha"

w c n t [english horn] stop s

au [twang sound] h v o is

to [twang sounds] j o p is

cra [twanging sound] k p u is

tic [twanging'd] j u g is is

li [spilling water sound] h s r

ti [spilling water sound] p l s

g [spilling water sound] g d s

ant [spilling water sound] m a ma

in

[bongos play] y v e singing

noc [bongos play] t t p t

u [bongos play] slap up saying two loud'r

lated [bongos play] cracking finger p t

co [plates crashing down] g r w

ro [plates crashing] walls' bend j o

na [crashing walls] in flat r r

ry [walls collapsing] flat r r r

fur [scuffing shoe sounds] peel it a

ni [scuffling shoe sounds] left foot edge

tur [scuffling shoe sounds] and h r

e [scuffling shoe sounds] v y e

tel [wind howling sounds] window o p

evis [wind howling sounds] toss't o p

ion [wind howling sounds] smash t j

s [wind howling sounds] wind howling sounds

la [dripping water] pt pt a p

mp [dripping water] pt pt a psh

sh [dripping water] pts pts pst pst

ade [dripping water] phst ps pts p

phen

[chewing sounds] assumptions h t s

o [chew sound] fifty fifty'z v q

men [chew sounds] unless h four k

a [chewing chewy] it's f ork t

per [crunch gravel] tastes good rm a

gut [crunchy gravel] s 2 inch 1

tor [crunch sands] d wit f ork

easies [crunchy sandwich] sprout n lettuce s

ground [sing birds] h o gk checkers

ed [birds singing] hall way d w

flow [bird sang] hand v e top

ed [birds chirp] s by hand print

in [ultra sound] handles grip wrists band

cred [ultra sounds] twist hand grip up

i [ultra sounding] banging s t against

ble [ultra sound ed] poles tall g

dr [splashing] but g a were grv

op [slash around] j o h arm

pi [splashes] round corn r s street

ng [slashes] tendons first up s i

the [sucking whirs]

real blade a s

chuck [sucks whir] slice r y e

ling [whirring suck] s no blood no

s [whir sucking] fall pack't d oh

fetis [scratch s] g t o f

his [scratch ss] v s l k

tic [scratch] x r e f

s [scratch] c o r k

syn [flushing] ring b t pipes out

the [more flushing] pipe r t rings

size [flushes] look over g two sets

t [flushings] banging rattle'd r ringing s

drag [burping] dense forest f o tr

n [burp] thin sandy s a r uh

e [burping mud] let s long line

t [burp] short t grasses t out

con [] legs g f torn d

stella [] arms f g ripped s

t [] heads hf g rolled y

ion [] eyes hfg see out f

bit

[helicopter blades] tin run f e

ter [blades] g d l s o

s [helicopter blades] b g bronze s

m [blades] slashed f grasses y down

bliss [ringing] hello put f on auto

t [rings] what that's creamy spinach a

er [ringing phone] butter n bread'd garlic

ing [ringing phones] riso b g b

al [drips] one more f a has

a [dripping] needles drop s d is

ba [drippers] little splash g up t

ma [drip] brooms f e t er

a [popping] since t f h o

t [poppings] then g d e u

l [pop] there wasn't y f a

a [popping] then could h s y

la [barking] x g two dogs m

can [barks] b o forms opposite each

ian [barkings] symbo et 'lusion j on

s [barkers] nism s anthro bites h

fu

[cheers] begs one c e j

tua [cheering] growing h u r a

r [cheers roar] t's break v n

al [cheer] o'ss where at y r

go [silence] o mention s g to

mr [silences] pencil after as erase buts

inger [silencers] six added c t o

s [silenced] as 7 fall off gn

easter [shutters] tag d y t where

ings [shutterss] tags e x u there

an [shuttering sound] thumb f y r

gel [shutter] thumbs g c s tr

an [unzip sounds] eats a bit bit

ham [zip fast sound] entropy a bit

fin [zippers louder] j eats j bit

lay [zzzzip] mil o me bit r

ro [saw] foam n g f h

gert [saw] foamy that h r s

horn [saw] foamys r of low air

hill [saw] splaying at gravel h r

en [ring sounds]

slaps against h w

tro [ringing sounds] slapping as t r

pee [rings] slap slap bear splash it

s [ringer sounds] roll over slap t

tri [uneasing beat] some one r g

an [uneasing sound] another big dot here

gl [uneasing beats] h d r t

es [un easing beater] forgets word h

look [rev sound] eye turn t w

a [revs sounds] leg over b p

wry [revving] arm pinned c o

m [revving sounds] arms crossed stop there

d [peck] pore g fy trip s

rif [peck] pinned g fy since t

t [peck] pulse g fy then m

s [peck] halls f gy of or

w [smacking lips] placed n circles how

his [smacking] dropped n no arrange mt

per [smacking lips] one tree a g

s (smacking lips) where b t reach

re

[low menacing music] parts sung up

pel [low menacing music] helped b ex

ant [low menacing music] sawed left over

s [low menacing music] drip to drip

e [distant rumblings] part blue hare to

cho [distants rumbling] k g r greener

ing [distant rumbles] goats w hr a

s [distancing rumble] yellow s h p

re [overlapping clatter] h d us y

pre [overlapping] pay back s weight m

sent [overlaps] the ways look for c

ed [overlap] pushy w n d er

sea [crackling fire] broken bone s ar

son [fire cracks] slash t rake t

a [crackling] g o de rs

lick [fire] b e s n d

nu [devoid noise] v d u q

ou [devoided noise] practical j r a

ve [devoided noise] tens after hour s

au [devoid noise] c r p s

rob [puckering sounds]

ground head in p

be- [puckering sounds] p head ground in

grill [puckering sss] head in p ground

d [puckering sounds] ground head p in

cun [hissing propane] concrete erosion a b

ni [[hissing propane] ate mints o w lp

ngh [hissing] 'cillates scio s blocks stk

am [hiss] n stab i l ty

y [atomism taps] east sun rise d

ou [atomism tap] tapped trop ica na

n [atomisms] corner s tr n fast

g [atomism taps] turn r d up

fra [bug buzz] ball s do bounce

gme [bug buzz] an apprehension s off

n [bugs buzzing] flat floor thirty degrees

ted [bugs buzz] wall then wall floor

flo [] not motion d r d

w [] b w drag t dirt

e [] started as zero s crash

rs [] desire s j o sack

sp

[tire flaps] plain h u tucked

on [tires flap] slow n gravel there

ge [tire flapping] and j st in

s [tire flaps] any dust d v kl

ve [metal banging] b i r y

c [metal banging] we're up sell it

tor [metal banging] v et op rolling

ng [metal banging] bad foot split hoof

[gas rumble] one item put it down

[gas rumble] seconds in through h k

[gas rumbles] days later water pours t

[gassy rumbling] week day filter d a

s [bang] run run run run run

h [bang] run run run run run

o [bang] run run run run run

t [bang] run run run run run

bubble s r i takes off blooms

drip water drop s t p er

little finger wave r o still though

((((which)))) ((((brings)))) splash tails b n p

one movement

s h t [pats] tense

grab't "come on" carrying up some steps

"grab't" b z left turn s r

d next move weak leg motion s

A long line of ants broken by small stones;

Margaret and June poking the ferns. June says "what happened?"

Margaret turned. Ants, a long line. Broken by the small rocks.

Margaret says "it's a dead rabbit."

derivative bend they've borrowed drop s around

one break drugged r fit that t

have b r k filling in cracks

round some back track d dirt s

chop slice and roast d "sure, buddy"

direct no [noises] more question d a

held detachment d left levers "a duck"

12 signs [knock] ng pulled from over't

tree each side miles ckritu

"chained to a wall" bleed drop out

r [saw] wall s "cans" vgtsm spent

[truck] spin s gas g n t

pallet

[knocks on door] pregnant wall 2
five (ings) [knocks] sacks down rd
rise up [knocking] pulls set r off
a little "don't take it back, again."
[engine turns off] "where does" it take
that Margaret looked at June "carpet" where
small dots [engine] shift base "have" there
arm s key drops "it" need I

A song

At home

I'm legal
I'm white
I'm male
I love my ar15
I love my ar15

G D G C D G

[engine running]

tear drop s weak laughter

June looked down, "another one," silent h

d g f [engine] trig'd Margaret "stop

poking" isn't protecting v top brick els

fact to June says, "there, on the"

a con-crete corner difference in one depths

s g t small bruising June "ow"

Margaret "what?" g t s "what?"

phone [rings] Margaret clomps the wooden stairs

[slam] screen door g t "hello?" uh

June turns sense t by the bay

"stay away" heel s taken low light

Jack said "June" tapped bottle once t

a through the high r parts eyes

track t g r lower voice d

"hey, June" slips backwards s in to

[dog barking] Jack's hand grabbed hair h

f k Margaret clomped down the wooden

stairs yelling "FOR YOU!" June fell t

but knees s k r p Jack

asphalt burn

[screaming] p t k ugh

er [screaming] late layer d s and

pitch d June with head s [screaming]

Margaret runs drive way v [screams] it

once forget d a [crack] whip s

that old train [whistle] float s o

v r foggy [shout] skin d elbow

head wounds [burp] regurgitate d ps a

[paranormal bangs] stick pump s start rattling 'gid h r t [paranormal

banging]

start d up "not often" or stopped

[paranormal bangs] cut t h other s

marigolds kill [dog panting] s start pump

[wheezing] rattling 'gid h r t [panting]

June's face plant dirt loose r leaf

s [dog panting] slap slap ng away

"no beans" and John sit t wall

there dark angle [glasses clink] one eye

ye "no, no beans" [plates clinking] head

back "look no beans, rice" right hands

[back crack]

Margaret pulled June loose hose

[crackle] leave s [clomp] June [screaming] of

once or two bend t r s

Margaret [sobs] get one if it e

[bubbling sound] one more "bet it" tried

[bubbling sound] one more puncture d tr

[bubbling sound] "hey, two to 1" h

zzzz [bubbling sound] say "hi" r that

[shots] two of "tip it" though

[shots] scar s of slashe d trs

[shots] "ya, three to 2" t

ssss [shots] say "bah" k but o

[ringing lines] pain June is dragged up

steps [thunder rolling] pain Margaret's arm b

a [chickens chicken] pain cry tear s

f [talking] pain Margaret June hug t

away s [clinking] Jack up out "uh"

scrap d so spaces [clinking] chairs away

on wood floor "what..." away s carry

d Jack's bike ng away street [clinking]

[taps]

one addiction each j u s

t [tapping] ground where "that's gas!" tooth

juggle Jack walks "it's a" [taps tap]

left of brick v o b a

Margaret chokes [cough] June's leg n at

"sell it" two more thorn s ex

d a [cough] leg June at once

Magaret chokes [coughing] leg at over et

[spitting] Jack's coat out y e leather

lather [spit] break s out blow ng

matter [spitting] "oh, palms'" h drop s

cotton pants [spit] back staring is up

[woops] at one end Jack's bk o

land [woops] rolls floor oak back s

[woops] a knee a fist an "poke

n eye" slid for wards Jack's backt

[talking] bits "whispering" Jack sees [talking] non

glass shards "converging" [drone] ng layer s

leaves [talking] eye open one of "'nited"

g [talking] s roam even a hand

[

[b c

check what [screech] bird s f y

tongue doggies [screech] r sqrl s out

[screech] the door s open d m

licks t dirt s [screech] whis els

[plinks] g r cans u answer t

steadily [plinks] f a ulate r s

[plinking] "issues" one more 'tence t b

"up out or" [plink] for m r

"meaning" alone [steps] s 1 overt t

obert' that saying "one" count's out d

d returns "and" p derive t more

to [steps] or aspects no one'd a

a 'zome [hums] neither t d r

[hums] "see?" once h thought was

pumps bitter [hums] "see" spread't b

r [hums] not close r 'anged d

tongue doggies

[ssss] r sqrl s out

check what [ssss] bird s f y

licks t dirt s [ssss] whis els

[sssst] the door s open d m

drop't dropper [slice] tomatoes skin d

carrot s ta [slice] d p or

a pepper'd back "part one" ice d

floors a carrot a fall floor t

cucumber s ta [slice] d p or

a pepper'd back "oh isolated" ice d

drop't dropper [slicer] fing r skin d

floors a fall floor a cucumber t

Jack walked [chirps] sat b t for

minute "the bar" grab t hand out

[chirps] "the bar" away corner right before

Jack's between [chirps] inside t barrel

"what things" flat shovel't clay y soil

[sish] f r i t has never

"what thing" [sish] shovel d turn r

plays 2 to 1 two inches down

a pickup truck

[gurgling] Jack lifted bed

s g up r same bed

"as before" v r m os o

a pickup truck [gurgling] dump t to

robins bathed in the bird bath

two robins were eaten by coyotes

three tohees landed water at least up

flew get [block] test field s k

Jack rolls "saint peter!" s ome o

can't y break y "saint peter!"

ne choice many s arms bloody d

John rocks t y "saint peter!" skin knees

[crushing skull sound] "we all do" m

o ways t wall Jack ex t

[crushing skull sound] "there" did it a

s h burns hillside't down cycle s

[song ends] inner arm t drop d

ash "Levi's" [song ends] ride n up

or no burn s "cotton" balls death

[song ends] Jack's back y c back

[bbbbb] soon

stream bd s tug becomes

brawl [bbbbb] rocks there no random g

dilate of tink s roaring rushing on

a flat space [bbbbb] over roll down

[plosives] north south north Jack see s

nothing [plosives] g s y r turner

"pops" north one south r Jack s

body bagger s r t truck it

turn [branch break] crash t Jack kneels

ankle y e a two o

[branch break] bone scrape d open drip

around on round d crash d ground

darkness arrives painted flag [clap] n d

c genome Jack piece d [clap] out

s finite d capacity [clap] break d

n s "pow!" [clap] Jack passed out

feeling hell "more" [crapping] Jack k k

[crapping] flow d reverse s hell s

k k Jack senses "more" [crapping] d

eyeball 'shion roll s roll s

[music ends]

Jack's eyes roll r back

no another t [music ends] or 'nother

limes cupped 'ratives non as "hey, Jack"

[music ends] no thing t that Jack

[shouting] "fires" s drug s give

Margaret [shouting] June s face d

roll it over [shouting] "here" drink this

Margaret say s [shouts] what d this

catch it "see" [dry wind] blowing trees

Margaret wraps wounds t e June "see"

[dry wind] cries f s down in't

tree t r left Margaret a "see"

linked m over a or [salty airs]

"molar" s tope not link t in

[salty airs] d sionless one two 3

"molar" rent d is o mix tr

big "local" one minute s Margaret tense

d [forks] break d bark s "local"

[forks] 'stand es o t June s

tense "local" what s matter of t

end note

leaves rustle em quiet r planes overhead r

bird s forgotten t 1:05 pause m hums light rs

breath —,— together separate empty

d room fill t wasn't there s noise isn't stupid r

harry k stammer is a writer, musician and painter who lives and works in Santa Barbara, CA USA. His books include *every beyond't nothing* (persistencia), *tents* (Otoliths), *grounds* (Otoliths); and *tocsin* (Otoliths), *sidewalkss* (Concrete Mist Press), *walls't's* (Sandy Press), *-48* (Sandy Press) and *alleys't'* (Concrete Mist Press). Recent noise/poetry pieces are available at http://harrykstammer.bandcamp.com